A SHELTER AFTER THE STORM

Bettie Bears Skelton

ISBN 978-0-557-56841-3

Dedicated to all of those who
Served,
Gave,
Prayed
during and after Katrina and Rita
and especially to
those evacuees who were our guests at the
Arkansas Baptist Assembly in Siloam Springs, Arkansas,
during September and October, 2005

FOREWARD

On September 3, 2005, we became part of an extraordinary experience in service. That was the day that I called our City Administrator and asked what our church could do to assist in the caring for hundreds of Hurricane Katrina evacuees from New Orleans who were due to arrive at a Bible camp outside our small Northwest Arkansas community.

That call led to my becoming part of the Operations Team. At the same time, Wendell led our church's response and its adoption of a family from Mississippi.

It was a whirlwind month, filled with emotion, wonderment, disappointments, new friends, new understandings, new relationships and a new appreciation of the resilience of the human spirit and the ability of an entire community, state and nation to respond to the desperate needs of their neighbors.

The first evening of the camp, Tuesday, September 6, I came home tired, emotionally drained, hungry, my mind full of the incredible experiences of the day. Not wanting to lose the memories and to serve as an emotional outlet, I went to the computer and started writing my thoughts. As I wrote I realized there were friends and family who would appreciate these experiences so I e-mailed what I had written to them.

Then the power of the internet took hold. I immediately heard from many who had received Day 1 and almost everyone reported they had forwarded it to other friends and that they could hardly wait for Day 2. So it became a part of my daily life—writing my diary and musings and sending them out to who knows where.

Ultimately, these daily writings became a tool that was used to bring financial support to a Katrina family who has settled here in the community and who today is a contributing part of our town. I also hope that the writings were an influence in the decision of several to participate in work trips to the hurricane areas to assist in the recovery efforts.

As you read this journal please remember that this is truly a journal. I wrote as I observed and as I felt at that time. It is not history although it has some historical value. Those who were there are sure to have observations different from mine. They have their own perspective and they would tell a different story. It would be incredible to put them all together.

I wish I had pictures of the camp to share with you. But early on the leadership made the decision that cameras were off limits. A good decision that provided the evacuees with a degree of privacy and respect.

Now it is five years after Katrina and Rita and the Gulf Coast is dealing with another catastrophe. This one is different and the oil spill has not created the flood of instantly homeless people as did the hurricanes. It is bringing devastation differently but in a way that may be just as life-changing and long lasting. We have yet to learn what kind of assistance we may need to provide.

We extend our appreciation to all of our friends and family, those whom we met through this experience and those who have stood by us throughout a lifetime of involvement.

It is my hope that you will find within these pages the inspiration to take on your own ministry of service. For us it was only a phone call away, the willingness to make the phone call, and the determination to say yes.

Bettie Bears Skelton

July, 2010

Siloam Springs, Arkansas

Tuesday, September 6

Day 1

Dear Friends,

Where do I start to tell about my day? This was the day when Siloam Springs became the temporary home for 535 people displaced by Katrina. I want to write about it because I want to always remember this day and this week.

Let me back up. There is a large Baptist campground here that holds about 900 kids a week during the summer. It had been designated awhile back as a Red Cross shelter. We have known since last Friday that up to 900 evacuees could be coming here after being at Fort Chaffee in Fort Smith for a day or so.

Our involvement began when I called the City Administrator last Saturday to see how our church could help. He ended up asking me to join the City team as the Team Leader for Faith-Based Operations. That responsibility is to mobilize the city's churches in volunteer efforts. And Wendell is leading our church's Disaster Response Team. We spent the Labor Day weekend getting organized and getting prepared. Most of us are complete amateurs at this.

We finally got the official word this morning that we would be receiving around 600 people mid-afternoon. At 3:00 I was at Trinity Pentecostal Church of God which is about 1/4 mile north of the campgrounds. We had decided to use it as the place for volunteers to receive their orientation and then to be bused to the camp. Well, someone wisely decided this was also a good place for the buses carrying the evacuees to come first and then, as people were processed, be moved bus by bus into the camp. I was talking to a volunteer and she said, "Here they are." We looked up and saw 7 large Greyhound-type buses pulling into the church parking lot--the second wave of evacuees. They circled the lot and parked one behind the previous one; each seat of each bus occupied by someone who today has nearly nothing and two weeks ago had lives that in most ways were similar to ours.

What a special moment that was! Then the first buses began their short journey from the church to the camp and we waved to the passengers (whom we could not see through the dark glass). My heart was in my throat and I was close to tears as I realized that these people were now dependent on us getting it right.

An hour later I went into the camp and was amazed at the quietness, the orderliness, the good spirit that I felt. I talked with one man who loved the beauty of the camp and another who couldn't believe our mountains--of course, there are no "mountains" around the camp--just a few hills. But I guess when you lived in New Orleans any hill looks like a mountain. He was scared of "those wild animals among the trees--bears, snakes, bobcats, possum." So we took a walk and discussed the small probability of those animals showing up.

Five hours and fifteen minutes after the first bus arrived all were processed and assigned a bunk in a building. They had clean linen, a pillow, a blanket, a towel and washcloth, soap, a toothbrush and toothpaste. Each building has 3 showers, 3 toilets, 2 sinks and bunks for up to 23 people. Some buildings will not have that many because families will not be separated.

But such an incredible response from every church and every person to whom I have talked this week. I have not approached one person or church who has said, "No, we can't." In fact, just the opposite. It has been, "What else can we do?" We have to stop accepting donations of clothes, food, bedding tomorrow because we have so much we have no place for it. Just cash for now. We have a database of thousands who want to volunteer. Churches are providing vans and drivers to transport volunteers (no cars on the campgrounds). A clinic has been set up on-site with round-the-clock professional staff to attend to health needs. A job fair is being planned for people who want to stay in the area. Already, a few people have been reunited with their families and have left the camp. We had to open the Community Center to receive donations, categorize them, and box them. Volunteers were abundant to staff this area.

Now, you understand that Siloam Springs is a town of 10,000-max. So this was a Northwest Arkansas-Northeast Oklahoma undertaking and what an outpouring!

Oh, it isn't perfect. We've already had to have Security break up a couple of domestic squabbles and someone was upset because a policeman shook his hand while wearing gloves. We learned that communication is a problem (isn't it always?) and a newsletter announcing the time of availability of FEMA and other agencies is vital.

But we're in it for the long haul. However, the camp isn't heated so if this goes on more than through October heat will have to be added. I hope we have as many volunteers six weeks from now. Or will the excitement turn to weariness and lose the appeal to stick with it? I guess that is our job--to make sure volunteers get the essential R and R.

On Thursday I meet with the Ministerial Alliance to discuss how to meet the spiritual needs that are present. Worship services on grounds or bring the people into existing churches? Ministers on-call or on-site all of the time? So many decisions.

An amazing day. I won't forget it. But for the first time in over a week, these people have a place to stay until they can make permanent plans. They're warm, clean, clothed, nourished, and welcomed. They have so much more than they did two days ago.

What a privilege I had today.

Bettie

Wednesday, September 7

Day 2

Dear Friends,

The first night went well. People slept. No arrests. What more could we ask?

When I walked on the campus of the camp this morning at 7:45, it was so quiet. It reminded me of church camp right before the morning bell rang. Peaceful. Full of anticipation.

The day was incredibly smooth--considering. We tried to stop accepting donations of things but, as you know, you can't stop a tidal wave and the stuff kept coming. Neither I nor my cohort had the courage or the insensitivity to tell a person who had driven 40 miles that we couldn't accept that load of clothing she had lovingly cleaned, folded, categorized and boxed. So we took it and still more came. Tomorrow we really will have to stop taking it. We have filled all of the available space (almost) in the town. We have to use this wonderful surplus that God has given us before we take in more.

There are a few things we missed. Not enough trash cans. No way for mass communication--no p.a. system. Not even bullhorns. We had not anticipated so many people wanting to travel into town or people wanting to get to the bus station or airport so they could get to wherever their new home is. So we were short of transportation and that became a new part of my job description.

Was there ever a camp that didn't have a "Snack Shack"? Well, ours does, too. McKee Products which has a big bakery in Gentry, just a few miles north, has completely stocked the Shack with Little Debbie's products, and there is bottled water and sodas. All at no cost of course. That is where it differs from my camping days.

There are 110 kids who will report to the Siloam Springs schools on Monday. The school officials will be on-site to meet with parents on Friday and we hope to send each child to school on Monday with a new backpack and school supplies. Imagine being in that child's place. I don't think the first day of school will be a lot of fun.

A couple of stories that I don't want to forget: I was talking with the woman who is coordinating the distribution of clothing at the camp to see if she had any special needs. She told me that a man had come in who wore size 50 and they could not find a thing within the donated clothes to fit him and she asked what she was to do. I, using all my learned administrative skills, said I would get back to her. I walked back up the hill and my phone rang. It was a woman from Dayspring Cards (their headquarters are here) and she was calling to report some information. She asked if there was anything else she could do. After about a nanosecond, I said, "How would you like to adopt a man who wears size 50 and we have not clothes for him?" Well, of course, there was no question about it. She left work, went to Wal-Mart, bought the clothes, and had them to him 90 minutes later. She told me later that she sent out an e-mail to some of her colleagues and the money to pay for the clothes was there in minutes.

She also said that one of the volunteers had told her the campers were asking for 2005 calendars. Another of those things we take for granted. Within a matter of minutes she had 19 on her desk. Then she found among the Dayspring staff several dozen two-year planners and they were soon in the hands of those who needed them.

But my story of the day goes like this: I was at the gazebo (kind of a gathering place) this evening and a man came up to me and said, "I got a job!" So I rejoiced with him and it seems that he worked for a cement company in New Orleans and worked with a man who later moved up here. They made contact and the man here got him a job with his company. He starts tomorrow and he needed for me to find him a pair of work shoes. So we went to the clothing trailer and found a fairly good pair of work shoes, size 12. Except that he is a 10. He said he could wear them tomorrow and would I get him some size 10's tomorrow. I said I would (not having a clue where they were coming from) and I asked if they should be steel toed. "Yes," he said, "and above the ankle." I gave him my cell phone number so he could check with me when he got back from work on Thursday. Later I decided it was time to go home. I had to stop at Trinity Pentecostal--the church I told about yesterday where all the buses stopped--and leave some things to help register volunteers tomorrow. I got there just as they were starting their evening service and I decided this would be a great time to say thank you to the congregation. The pastor agreed and during my little talk I told the above story and asked if anyone had size 10, steel-toe, above the ankle work boots to please let me know.

14 minutes later, a man walked up to me carrying size 10, steel-toe, above the ankle work boots. He said, "They're pretty dusty. I've been carrying them around in my truck for a long time." Why am I surprised when God works this way?

These are the encounters that will keep us going, will lift us up when we are oh, so tired.

Several people are already leaving the camp as they contact family and friends. That is good. I don't know if we will get more people in or whether our numbers will be allowed to decline. Whichever, we're ready.

This is an ideal place for people to re-locate. Our unemployment rate is under 4%. Employers are scrambling to snatch up the skilled workers in the group. A job fair is being planned and should be something to see.

Wendell spent most of today obtaining housing for one of the families that our church adopted--not from the camp. He was successful and by the end of the week they will have a 3-bedroom house with a basement, filled with donated furniture. And the man of the family has a job with Allen Canning. They wanted him to start today.

I'm talking with the local Ministerial Alliance tomorrow to get their ideas about how to incorporate worship services into the life of the camp. We've learned there are at least two ministers among the 540. They organized today to have a worship service tonight. I wish I could have attended. I wish I had thought to ask them to attend the meeting of ministers in the morning. I will get their input before we set up any worship opportunities. I will make an opportunity for them to meet with local ministers.

Well, it is 11:40. Time to get to bed. Day 3 is just ahead. Oh, yes, our City Administrator who is in charge of this whole thing asked that we begin our Team meeting this morning with prayer. He led it. I could tell he was not a stranger to praying. Gives you confidence and hope.

Good night.

Bettie

And thanks to all of you who sent such encouraging notes. They were.

Thursday, September 8

Day 3

Dear Friends,

We knew today would happen. It always does. Tempers were flaring, communications broke down, misunderstandings arose, territorial issues began to rise, and frustration grew with state and federal governments. And that was just among the staff! I guess we are tired. Some have been at this a week since the first word was received that people were coming. I've just been at it since Saturday but I'm tired. And my responsibilities are just a small part. But most of us went home early (or earlier) tonight. I'm going to sleep tonight and not do anything foolish by trying to resolve some issues while I am tired. I'll pray some more tonight and God will show us through these difficulties. We really appreciate the notes from so many of you that you are praying for us. That keeps us going!

But there were lots of good things today. First off, I met with the Ministerial Alliance What a group of guys! All who were at the meeting were pretty energetic people and eager to be of assistance. When I told them there were some ministers among the guests (that is what I am trying to call the evacuees now) they were eager to meet them and find out what THEY wanted/needed from the local ministers to support them. I was so proud of them for taking this approach rather than saying, "Look, this is what we'll do." So a group of local ministers came to the camp this afternoon to speak with the ministers. First I should tell you a little about these 3 guests who are ministers. They have already established themselves as leaders among the group and gracious leaders they are. I wish I knew a little more of their personal stories. Maybe later. They talked and decided to have a Protestant service in the morning and a Catholic service in the afternoon. The churches will also run vans to the camp so that anyone who wishes to can go into town to worship services. Our local ministers are taking them to breakfast tomorrow morning. So it was a good experience for everyone--brother finding common ground with other brothers.

Tonight, as I was leaving, I heard singing. Not far away the minister-guests were holding a worship service in one of the camp shelters. I and my companion, the head of the counseling department at John Brown University, wandered over and joined in the singing. It turned out that this was the end of their service and when they saw us (we did stand out in the small crowd!) they insisted on introducing us and having us say a few words. The warmth with which they received us was exhilarating. We prayed together and I think that the joy these people showed is incredible in the face of what they have experienced.

We did stop donations as planned. But that is pretty hard for people to understand. Hopefully, when we need donations later (if we do) people will respond and not be offended that we cut them off now. We have large corporations wanting to take on complete projects. That is good but I try to help them understand that individuals need to be a part of this effort and although a corporation could take a need and quickly turn it around, if the need is not urgent, we need to let others help.

I spent most of my day off the campsite so I didn't see O'Dell--the guy who needed the work shoes. He must have gotten them last night because he didn't call me. I take that as a good sign.

Tonight the NFL season started and they hooked up a big screen in the Worship Center. I would have loved to have been a part of that. I bet it was a fun time. I don't even know who played. It wasn't the Packers, was it? No, I'm not that far out of touch.

We don't have laundry facilities here. Remember this is a summer church camp and they don't launder clothes at camp. That has been an issue and most of the laundry now is being done at laundromats in town with people taking their dirty laundry in a bag, lugging it there on the bus, and bringing it back in a plastic bag. It would cost around $20,000 to build a wash area that would have 10 washers and 10 dryers. The cost is relatively low because it would be built on a site where there was once a building and the sewer is connected and the major work has already been done. The debate has been whether that is cost-effective given the length of time the camp may be open. Today the Ministerial Alliance said they would do a major fund drive for this project and the churches would raise as much as possible--which I think would be a great deal. They were eager to do it. I got the go ahead from the Camp Director and also learned that if I can get a couple of licensed plumbers and electricians to donate their time/supplies the cost can be cut by around $6000. God will give us these people and the money will be there. Now if any of you want to give.........

Looking back over this letter I see it sounds sort of down. It has nothing to do with the guests. It all has to do with politics--both governmental and non-governmental. Our Team on-site works very well together and I think we put the camp together in record time and with quality. Now, of course, others want to get in and tell us how to operate our house. This has been a great community outreach--a coming together for a common cause. And there is room for everyone to have a role in helping. It will be a long time until it is over. This is only Day 3 since arrival. We need to re-focus. I need to re-focus.

By the way, I'm learning to be thankful for things I never thought of being thankful for: cell phones, pockets, short hair, golf carts, chairs. When you work without an office these things are essential.

In summary: the thing that really counted today and keeps us ready for tomorrow is seeing families reunited. Seeing people leave because they are reunited with their families and friends. That is the whole thing.

But tomorrow should be fun. Red Cross and Social Security will be here to write checks. The banks will be here for them to be cashed. We expect a lot of people will then have the means to leave. I guess it is too late today to buy Wal-Mart stock. Too bad, when these checks arrive Wal-Mart will have a banner day. There will be a lot of shopping going on! I can identify with that.

Until then,

Bettie

Friday, September 9

Day 4

Dear Friends,

It must have been the prayers that made Day 4 a complete turnaround from Day 3. And that is good! Really good! Maybe it is because God led me this morning to a lovely place to work from-the front porch of a cabin at the camp, kind of away from the busyness, shaded by beautiful black walnut trees that are just beginning to shed their leaves, and quieter. You see, none of us have offices at the camp. That is good. But it is sometimes tricky, talking on a cell phone in one hand, a pen in the other, and holding a notepad on your knee. So I spent a couple of hours this morning working from my new office. It was great.

I came out of our staff briefing this morning at about 9:00 and walked down the path to the East of the cafeteria and I was more than startled to see straight ahead an officer dressed in a navy blue uniform, standing there grimly holding, what looked to me like a sub-machine gun. Everything looked pretty quiet to me. I finally decided to approach him and ask what was going on (I had identification on my shirt--I'm not completely stupid.) I asked if we had a problem and he responded, just like in the movies, "No, Ma'am, we're trying to prevent one." I then noticed a new bus had been set up nearby. I inquired of a man standing by what was going on and he told me this was the new bank. Then I remembered that this was the day that Social Security checks were being handwritten and also Red Cross was giving emergency money. All of the local banks had been invited (really asked) to be there to allow people to open accounts. The bank bus, though, was there to immediately cash the checks. I know there was a lot of money around but I thought the gun was a little much. I thought all we need is for a rogue TV camera to make it on the campus and film an armed guard standing there! I did notice that he left a little later so I suspect someone with more authority than I thought the same thing.

The distribution of money went very well, I believe, and it will speed the guests on their way. At least those who have a place to go. Of course, many haven't yet seen FEMA. Who has? But they are supposed to be here next week and a lot of people don't want to leave until they have actually talked with FEMA, and hopefully gotten that money.

Wendell has been working as hard as I with the work of our church's disaster response. I am so proud of this church because of what they have done. They have already adopted 2 families and are considering a third--not from the camp. Adopting means helping them with everything--finding a house, furniture, jobs, reaching the social agencies, getting enrolled in school, everything you do when you move and a lot more.

I may have told you about the woman from our church, Roni, who decided to take a trailer of gasoline to Mississippi a week or so ago. Well, she did. I think some JBU students accompanied her so she was not alone. When she got there she met a family who had no place to go so she called her husband and told him she was bringing them back--4 people--parents and 2 kids. Her husband called the church and the whole thing was set in motion. It was learn as you go but Wendell and his team did a great job. They move into their 3-bedroom home this weekend that will be completely furnished. He has a full-time, permanent job with Allen Canning. God is good!

But the really interesting thing out of this is that Chica may get a baby sister. When Roni was in Mississippi someone walked up to her and handed her a little Westie dog and said, "Please see that she gets a good home." Roni already has 6 dogs and that is about her limit and the family she brought back with her cannot have pets in their new home. Roni kept telling Wendell how cute she is and he finally met her today. So we will probably adopt her. She is trained, responds well to commands, and Wendell says she is a very good dog. We had been talking about getting Chica a playmate--someone to stimulate her as she gets a little older. So this is probably it. Right now she (not Chica) is being treated for a bladder infection (no surprise). Any thoughts on a name? We could give recognition (no prizes) for the best name submitted. We won't call her Katrina, though.

We have now identified 4 ministers among our guests. I may have mentioned yesterday that a group of ministers from Siloam Springs were taking them to breakfast this morning. I'm not sure what all they did on that trip but it was a lot more than just breakfast. Everybody was in a van and after breakfast they toured the city to show them the churches, took them clothes shopping, and went to the local Christian bookstore. Saturday evening they will pick up the ministers and take them into one of the local Pentecostal churches for service (they're also picking up anyone else who wants to go) and on Sunday they will attend the First Christian Church in town. These preachers are really into this which makes my work a lot easier. I call the churches all of the time for vans/buses/volunteers and anything else I need and it is always, I mean always, there. Not a refusal yet.

My story of the day is about Gidget. This is a lot better than the gun story above. I got a call from the Department of Emergency Management guy at the camp this afternoon. He was frantic and did not have a clue what to do about this situation. Somehow, Gidget had gotten through to their office and told of her plight. According to him, she said she was in a Super 8 in Rogers (that is about 30 miles northeast of here and a pretty good sized town), completely broke, could not stay another night in the Super 8, but if she could get to Joplin, MO, her family would meet her there. Joplin is no more than 2 hours north of here. It was 4:00 and I knew there was a bus that left that area for Joplin at 7:45 PM (we've set up a route from camp to go to the bus station for that bus everyday). But I did not know a soul in Rogers who might take on this job. By the way, this woman had found her own way to Rogers. She is not one of our camp guests. I picked up the area phone directory and turned to the church yellow pages. My next thought was about what would be the church most likely to still have someone there at 4:00 on a Friday afternoon. My finger landed on First Baptist in Rogers. Aha! So I called and Vicki answered the phone. I told her the story, gave her Gidget's (can't believe that name) location, phone number, etc. I asked if her church would pay for her ticket to Joplin and get her on the bus. Vicki said, no problem, she would personally handle it. Well, the real story when Vicki talked to Gidget herself (that communications thing, again) is that she can stay until Monday at the Super 8, and her family can't pick her up in Joplin until Monday, and she has no money for food. By the way, the DEM guy had checked her out and she is a legitimate evacuee. When Vicki called me back she told me the real story and I asked if her church would adopt Gidget and see that her needs were met and that she got connected with her family. Vicki responded that she was just going to suggest that. As Vicki and I got acquainted she told me that she was the church's Disaster Response Coordinator and they were just trying to decide what they could do. They had prepared to receive some evacuees and they never came. So do you think my finger just happened to stop at First Baptist Rogers? And that Vicki just happened to answer the phone? I don't think so.

Most things will quiet down over the weekend. Agencies won't be on campus. We've closed the clothing store--where people have access to donated clothing--for the weekend, and just generally gear-down. It was an administrative decision to give guests and staff both some downtime. Good idea, I think. I'll go out for a few hours but we plan to have a short day there. But it is the first weekend so who knows how it will go. We think it will be fine.

Tonight was Siloam High's first home football game and Harvard Avenue Baptist picked up anyone who wanted to go. They'll experience Arkansas football which is pretty much an addiction in this part of the state.

We really appreciate the loving notes you are sending us. They keep us moving ahead. I am convinced that it was your prayers that kept us buoyed after hitting the wall yesterday (Is that a mixed metaphor?). Keep them coming, or rising--whatever prayers do. You are the wind beneath our wings.

Serving Him Together Through Serving Others,

Bettie

Saturday, September 10

Day 5

Dear Friends,

Notice that I'm not writing this at 11:00 PM. I actually came home about 4:00 after getting there this morning around 9:00. There was a lot of activity at the campsite today but mostly recreational stuff going on as almost all agencies were off the campus for the weekend. We had a lot of new faces among the volunteers as youth and college groups came to help out.

I saw in the paper last night a picture of a woman evacuee somewhere going through this huge mound of donated clothing. I want you to know that is not the case here. Our clothing store operates out of two large trailer units (the things I call "semi" trailers--I mean the really long ones). They are parked side by side and everything inside is in labeled boxes--men's clothing, women's shoes, toys, etc. Each day the clothing coordinator and her volunteers of the day set articles out on long tables in an organized fashion and people can come and select from the supply between 10:00 and 1:00. Sometimes there are special needs that have been identified and today they worked to fill those but did not open to the general population. Then each afternoon they put it all away until the next morning. I feel this is much more respectful to our guests rather than going through mountains of clothing. A good amount of what we are able to provide is actually new.

I looked back over my previous days' musings thinking that I had shared with you the Wal-Mart connection but I can't find it, soooo.... Do not ever trash Wal-Mart to me. This organization has been there beside us every step of the way. It, of course, is the main shopping environment for everything from food to tires in town so maybe they do have a greater responsibility. They have donated enormous amounts of prescription medications. Immediately after Day 1 regular bus trips into Wal-Mart were established and people go there every day. Of course they purchase items, too, and that is good for the company but they also stay there a long time and it fills a social need. Just a note, the Siloam Springs Wal-Mart was the 4th store opened by the company.

I don't think I have ever mentioned the weather. It has not rained for a couple of weeks which is really good for the camp but not so good for other things. Temperatures are in the high 80's to low 90's and lots of sun in the daytime. The humidity has not been bad and it gets chilly now at night--especially if you are used to the New Orleans heat and humidity.

I understand the trip into the football game last night was a real treat with a lot of mixing of the camp kids and the town kids. School starts Monday and I think everyone is prepared.

A couple of miracles today. Our Congressman approved $20,000 for 10 washers and 10 dryers to be purchased. The second miracle is that they will be installed by Tuesday. That will ease the work of the guests enormously because they either had to wash by hand or go into town to the laundromat. Not a good thing. We were so skeptical that this money was going to come that we were considering starting a drive among the churches to pay for it.

I'll close tonight with a quote from a Status Report sent to the Team today by our City Administrator, David, who has done an incredible job of holding things together. "Every day, astonishing reports of families being reunited with loved ones is overwhelming, some even bittersweet. For example, last night a young 17-year old adolescent, Cedric, went to the football game at the high school. When Cedric returned to the camp, he was informed that our team had located family in Colorado. One might imagine that Cedric would have been elated, not so. Cedric was devastated because he wanted to stay. That says so much about what is occurring at the Arkansas Baptist Assembly campground and our community. Cedric felt a sense of belonging and did not want to let it go."

Oh, I forgot, the Governor is probably going to attend worship services at the Campground. Would kind of be nice to be there but I really need to be in the church community tomorrow.

Tomorrow is 9-11. A day to remember.

The support of your prayers is almost palpable. I have run out of ways to say thank you.

Good night.

Bettie

Sunday, September 11

Day 6

Dear Friends,

This is Sunday, September 11, and I'm sure we all remember where we were 4 years ago and how our lives and hearts were affected that day. Katrina feels so much like it except there is no enemy with whom to go to war and release our anger. So we expend that energy on beating up our government for a slow response. I think it was slow but the analysis and assessing of blame must wait until these people are in safe places. What I had a hard time understanding is why the media, especially TV, with all of their resources could have not done more for the rescue effort. They were able to get into the devastated areas and report out. Was the reporting more important than taking the hand of a child and leading him to safety?

I did not go to the camp this morning and have only handled a few items via the phone. I thought it would be good to stay away a day. So my report on whether the governor was there for worship will have to wait until tomorrow.

So I would like to share with you a few other things.

My niece, Carmen, lives near Chicago. Besides being a mother of two small children, a wife, the music director for (I think) Junior High at her church, and giving piano lessons to a large number of budding musicians, is a consultant for Arbonne. She responded to one of my daily mailings and her signature reminded me that she did this. I asked her if Arbonne had skin and hair products specifically for African Americans. They don't but they have wonderful products and her colleagues have been challenged to bring at least one of their products to a meeting they are having next week to send to our guests here. Then, bright lady that she is, Carmen assessed her contacts and, another AHA! She used to teach music at an inner city girls' school in Chicago, where the predominant ethnic groups are African American and Hispanic. She contacted the Assistant Principal and the students will be collecting African American hair and skin products for our camp next week. Way to go, Carmen!

Our church, Community Christian Fellowship, an independent Christian Church, is the largest church in town with a weekly attendance of around 700. Our church leadership has adopted a ministry model of worshipping through service, with every believer serving others in the congregation, community and around the world. Today was the introduction of that model to the congregation. The introduction was so well presented and, of course, the timing was perfect as today was move-in day for our adopted family, Troy, Cora, Troy Jr., and Sharee. Tonight they are spending their first night in their new home and their first night together as a family alone (not in a shelter or someone else's home) for weeks. I just know that this will be a very special time for them. The house is fully furnished and equipped from donations by people from the church and very special friends of the church. The only thing that is missing is a dining table and chairs but even those have been improvised and that need will soon be met. Their rent is paid for several months until they can get on their feet. Wendell will help them next week to do things required by the state like car licensure, insurance, etc. Troy's job is 10 hours a day 4 days a week and comes with benefits so after 90 days they will have health care that is not Medicaid.

The kids start to school tomorrow (1st and 4th grades, I think) and their new principal saw them in church today and invited them all to lunch. Better than being sent to the principal's office, I would say.

The whole church becomes their support system and quite a lot of the community as well. Their next-door neighbor has donated considerable furniture and will be someone who looks over them very closely but not intrusively. He is on the staff at John Brown University and is active in the Baptist Church.

Roni and her husband have four kids and they have become good friends with Troy, Jr, and Sharee. What an example Roni and Galen have provided for their children these past weeks.

I guess this is a decent start to worship through service. But we can never out serve God. He continues to give and give.

And we brought our new little friend home with us today. She and Chica have cautiously explored each other and only moments ago I heard much ferocious noise from our bedroom. Wendell beat me there and he said he didn't know who initiated it, but I bet it was Chica. Some of you reading this may not know that Chica is our 10+ year old black, English Cocker Spaniel. We'll put our new family member in the bathroom tonight and shut the door. Good place for her since she still has her bladder infection. The vet told Roni she was about 2 years old. She is all white, of course, and the gunk that she was in for several days has stained her coat. Roni took her to the groomer who bathed her but did not cut her hair. They said that when they got her wet the odor was extremely bad and required a lot from them to get her clean.

We haven't decided on a name although Wendell leans toward, "Sister." Roni's kids were calling her Katrina. You have sent several suggestions. Gordon Venturella checked in with Stormy, Grace, and Windy. Judy Bilawa, who never sleeps, sent some from California at 3:35 AM: Dawn, Faith, Glory, Gracie or Gracious, Hosanna and Sister. My good friend Mary Lou Case, who is a lover of dogs, suggested Sally. She said, "I'd name her Sally, a nick name for Salvation. We are all reminded of salvation during crisis...". Such a big decision to make!

We will take her to the vet to have her scanned for an ID chip. We have one imbedded between Chica's shoulders that gives a contact number that is registered with the American Kennel Club. Since she is so well trained, and appeared well-cared for we thought she might have one and we will try to find her owners if that is so.

I think I will say goodnight now and get a longer night of sleep. Tomorrow's challenges will be there and it would be good to start the week rested. I have some things I would like to do this week that are "normal" things to do--a Missions Team meeting tomorrow night, teach diabetes and hypertension classes on Wednesday, and then this weekend there is a rug-hooking workshop at our church. I wonder if I'll be at any of them. I think so.

Sadness tonight--the Packers lost.

Continue to bathe all of us here in prayer. We know and feel it daily.

Bettie

Monday, September 12

Day 7

Dear Friends,

We learned this morning that the official census is 480 at the camp now. The official count to start with was 530, although we had been quoting 540. Just a little off, I guess. That 480 figure was a little disappointing as it felt like more than that had left the camp. But, the positive is that 50 people have found a new home with relatives, friends or in a new community. That is really pretty amazing. I think there will be more this week. A lot of resources were mobilized this weekend for faster travel--we had been mostly using bus transportation for people leaving. Now it will probably be direct bus to Houston and Baton Rouge which seem to be major portals for people to connect with others. Airplanes are being used where appropriate, such as the man today with multiple chronic health conditions who would not tolerate another long bus ride. But many will continue to use the commercial bus lines. Many people are used to traveling by bus or not go at all.

Governor Huckabee did come to the camp for worship services yesterday and my understanding is that it was an inspiring service. At the end of the service a woman resident-guest came up to the minister leading the service and asked where they should leave their tithe. The minister was rather taken aback and explained that they did not plan to take an offering due to the circumstances of the "congregation." She insisted because, "We want to give to help people get back to their homes." So the minister, realizing that this was important, told her they would put a container out and if people wanted to give they could. She was the first and then one by one people began to come forward to drop money in the container. Later when it was counted it was over $800.00. They gave out of their need; we give out of our abundance. The Widow's mite. So humbling. Such a testimony of love for each other.

I got a call this evening about a man who is working at Wal-Mart starting tomorrow at 7:00 AM. I think he may have been a Wal-Mart employee in New Orleans. The need was for transportation for him to get to work on time. That was no problem. We could fix that without even a phone call. But the caller's next statement was what got my attention. She said the man had a hearing impairment and he spoke sign language. That was the first I had heard of this man and I don't know how his need to communicate has been met up to now. I hope somehow this has been taken care of by someone. Tomorrow will be the day to check that out.

It is interesting to see the shift in focus among our leadership. Last week we were in crisis mode and everyone was putting out fires when they saw them flame-up. As a consequence, there was double work, not excellent communication, and all the issues that go with that--including short tempers. But the job was done and done very well according to those who have observed other shelters. This week, people are asking each other, "How can we do it better?" That is pretty healthy and I'm sure the organizational behavior people would say that this is consistent with the evolution of groups that quickly form to respond to a crisis. Is this what the various levels of government are going through, only we're doing it in microcosm?

Chica and her new sister had a very difficult night. Especially Chica. Especially Wendell and Bettie! Chica was very restless if we had her in bed with us. If we put her in a room by herself she barked. We put the new doggie in our bathroom with a nice soft bed, food, water, and a closed door. Remember the bladder infection? Just trying to protect the carpet. We kept them apart today but this evening they spent a couple of hours in the back yard at the same time and both are still alive. Wendell walked them both this AM--but separately. They both seem calmer tonight--so far.

About her name. Wendell liked "Lucky" as suggested by Cathey Everett, my 2nd cousin--a good name for obvious reasons. My god daughter, Janelle Nickerson (an English teacher) thought it would be good to make a connection with Chica's name which is Spanish for "little girl." She suggested that "Fifi" is similar in French and was continuing her research into the same meaning in Italian. But the new doggie is Scottish in origin and neither of us could think of the right term that a Scot would use. Her mother, Faye Bailey, the smart one, took a nanosecond to come up with "Lass." As Janelle said, "Duh..." So I'm lobbying for "Lucky Lass." What do you think?

I thought I would close tonight with a bit of poetry. I hope it, in some small way, conveys the many ways people show the caring spirit that so many have demonstrated since Katrina struck.

Caring is a mystery.
It has so many faces
It sometimes hides itself
And you think it's something else.

You think you're serving
When you give a cup of water.
And you never think that this
Is caring in disguise.

You think the joy you share
Is just a happy moment
And you never think that this
Is caring in disguise.

You think it is for love
That you lift him in his grief
And you never think that this
Is caring in disguise.

Serving, praying, joy and love
Faces of caring we see each day.
Filling our lives, touching each other
Passing it on in our Father's name.

Thank you for not only being able to care but living a life filled
with caring.

Good night.

Bettie

Tuesday, September 13

Day 8

Dear Friends,

The telephone awoke me this morning at 6:30. It was our van driver from one of the churches who is helping provide transportation. He was at the camp to take people to the Fayetteville bus depot to catch the bus to connections South, East and West. He went with a 15 passenger van and, with their luggage; he did not have enough room for everyone. We had to scurry around, get another van (thank goodness for our church!), get it out to the camp, load everyone up and get them to Fayetteville (about a 40 minute drive) by 8:15 to catch the bus. He made it although he admits to exceeding the speed limit. This is the first time that we have had this many leave at one time. As of last count today we have had 81 evacuees (15%) who have vacated the campground. That leaves 451 still there.

I told you yesterday about the $800+ offering that was taken at the camp's Sunday worship service. Well, today I took possession of all of that cash. The camp leadership decided to give it to the Ministerial Alliance (I'm not sure why) to use in some way for disaster relief at the camp. I think it was a good gesture because it meant the money did not stay in the hands of the people actually operating the camp and will bring the Ministerial Alliance closer to the operations of the camp. That is, if they ever see the money. Shortly after I got all of this cash I met the clothing coordinator and she said she needed to buy ponchos and umbrellas because of the rain forecast and where could she get the money. Imagine that. So she ended up with $250.00 of the offering money. This will come in so handy because occasionally we just need to buy something with cash. Cash still is easier than a purchase order, a credit or debit card. Then I called our minister and told him about the money and the portion that I had already spent. He will tell the other guys but he gave me absolution and told me to carry on. Whew!

Wendell and I are thinking about adopting a woman and her family whom I talked with today. She is living at the camp and instantly became a leader among the guests. She is, without a doubt, a people person. I watched her in action today and she is very capable of listening to others, calming them and helping them resolve their issues. I'm not the only one who has noticed this. She has actually begun helping officially in resolving camp issues. Her name is Rose and she has a 12 year old daughter (Erika), a 16 year old son (Roger) who are both in camp with her and a 25 year old son in college at Southern University in Baton Rouge who is finishing his BS in computer sciences. Most of her work career has been in clerical positions but just two weeks before Katrina she had started a new job as a Human Resources Director for a non-profit organization. She has an AA in Business Management and hopes eventually to return to school. She is probably in her mid-forties.

She wants to stay here. Her kids are already in love with the schools they are in and her son started football practice today--and that is the foremost reason she wants to stay. She needs a place to live--preferably a house so her son, for the first time in his life can have a dog--and have it furnished. She needs a job and she needs a car. Siloam has no mass transit since there is really no mass here to transport. This is the kind of family who will be an asset to this community. So we will probably adopt her. I don't think our church is quite ready to take on another family and we want to make sure Rose has the support she needs to make this transition successfully. To get a car, get set up in a house with donated furniture, incidental expenditures, and necessary deposits will probably cost about $6000, including covering her rent for 3 months--probably not more than $700.00/month.

Many of you have asked what you can do to help. Here it is. If we finally decide to do this (and I think we will) you can help with these expenses. Most of you who get this--at least on my original list as I have no idea how many times this letter is getting forwarded--can afford another $50.00 to help a specific family with a great work ethic, get a new start in life. You won't be sorry you did. Wendell has become an expert in this setting up of households for families who come with nothing. This will be the third one he has done--two for the church and Rose. If you would like to give toward her expenses in setting up her home you can write a check to Community Christian Fellowship Disaster Fund--that is our church--and mail to Skeltons at 19780 Shinn Springs Road, Siloam Springs, AR, 72761. Funny how I have become bold about asking for money. After this experience we have a different take on money and its purpose.

The resilience of the people here amazes and humbles me. While Rose and I were talking in the cafeteria a woman, about Rose's age, came up and asked her a question and the discussion became wide-ranging. However, it centered on the faithfulness of God, His steadfastness, the peace they experienced throughout all of this, the feeling that He is in control and all will be well. The faith they express is a life-lesson to me in itself.

We have so much to learn from them.

A couple of men were expelled from the camp for bringing a cooler of beer into the camp. They were given bus tickets to another location today and will not be allowed back in. That was a stupid, stupid thing to do as they were given the rules when they came into the camp.

There are rumors that President Bush is coming but we have heard nothing official.

There has been no rain for a couple of weeks and the camp is becoming dusty. A rain, except for the discomfort of being wet, would be a welcome visitor.

Good night,

Bettie

Wednesday, September 14

Day 9

Dear Friends,

It did rain last night, accompanied by a lot of thunder and lightning. I talked to our Camp Manager this AM and he did not believe that any rain came into the cabins. They have pretty wide overhangs. Still more rain in the forecast and it kind of showered off and on all day. It really cut the dust and that was a blessing.

I spent some time with Rose this morning and told her Wendell and I would like to take her and the kids to lunch Saturday, look at a house or two, and take the kids shoe shopping. She thought it was all a good plan and then said her kids had been wanting to go to a mall, which of course, Siloam Springs doesn't have--except about 100 strip malls--well maybe a few less than that. So I guess we'll take them over to Fayetteville to visit the NW Arkansas Mall. They're probably having withdrawal, having not been inside a mall for 3 weeks or so-- can any teenager stand that? She plans to go to the high school football game on Friday night. She said Roger, her son, will be on the sidelines the whole game as he won't be able to play until he has been with the team a few weeks. She says she doesn't know anything about the game except to yell and clap when the right color does something good. But Roger is a football fanatic. I told her that he would be interested in knowing that Wendell is a part owner of the Packers and she said that would totally overpower him. Should be fun.

We looked at a rental house for them and will show it to them Saturday afternoon. It is a 1928 house, well kept, 3 bedrooms and a bath upstairs, living and dining rooms downstairs and a small bath. The kitchen is pretty good with fairly new appliances and good flooring. It has a small yard and a storage shed in the back It has a back deck and a dandy front porch. Probably around 2000 square feet. It is right down town across from City Hall in a very nice neighborhood of older homes. It rents, I believe, for about $650.00/month and the owner will waive deposits. If Rose likes it we will get it rented ASAP and I suspect within a week we can have her and her family there.

Our thanks to all of you who have offered to support her. Our old home fellowship group (with some new members) in Downey, CA, wrote that they had prayed specifically Monday night for a way to become personally involved and then came Day 8. God doesn't waste time nor should we.

My diverse activities around the camp took a new turn today. The camp has continually been running out of ice and the days have been pretty warm. So someone donated 100 bags of ice a day. Nice and needed. One problem: the ice is at Wal-Mart and Wal-Mart does not deliver ice. Yesterday, someone brought it a few bags at a time to the camp. Not very efficient. So today someone decided we needed a better way and asked me to handle it. I called Wal-Mart and was told that the best way to load it would be from the pallet the ice was on to a flat-bed truck via a forklift. Great. I hardly know what a flat-bed truck is, let alone find one. I called Wendell. He had it solved within a couple of hours. He went to Allen Canning Company (they can vegetables--a pretty big company here in Siloam). He talked them into picking up and delivering the ice five days a week. Tomorrow the guy from Allen and I will go to Wal-Mart and walk through the procedure, take him out to camp, unload it and see how it works. Not exactly the "Faith-based Operations" I signed in for. But is it?

I do have a life outside the camp. I volunteer as an RN at St. Francis Clinic (providing health services for low-income-non-insured-people) here in town and last week I was all set to start some very badly needed classes/counseling on diabetes and hypertension. Well, that got blown out of the water with Katrina so I decided I had to start it today. I'm glad I did. I saw a few patients and felt good about being back in an environment where I felt very comfortable and knowledgeable and no one asked me to transport ice.

The camp organization continues to evolve. More people are added to the administrative staff as needs arise. Today a housing coordinator was added with a job of finding housing for people who plan to stay in this area on at least a semi-permanent basis. He is a volunteer, of course. Almost all of us are except those who have jobs with the city, county, etc. We did learn today that we would be reimbursed for our cell phone usage. Wendell said our bill so far is $35.00 more than usual. We never go over our plan. Up until now. I have really become acquainted with my cell phone. I was reluctant in the past to use it much. I think people should have some privacy and not always be available to anyone who wants to call. But communication would have been almost impossible without it these two weeks.

Good night. I'm having trouble hitting the right keys tonight. Maybe I should go to bed.

God's blessings on each of you.

Bettie

Thursday, September 15

Day 10

Dear Friends,

This has been an eventful day. So much, in fact that I had to write some notes so I will be sure to remember to write everything I want to tell you.

First, it rained. Our neighbor said it rained 1 1/2 inches. There were big puddles everywhere around camp but the little creek that runs through it didn't flood. It not only rained last night but all morning. When we started the day we thought there would be nothing going on today because of the weather. Wrong.

We have added a very special person to our list of recipients of this journal: Robert Jackson. Robert is Rose's son who is a senior at Southern University in Baton Rouge. I was telling Rose today about these daily reports and she wanted her son added. He is working for a newspaper part time and, she said, he wants to know as much as possible about the camp, the hurricane, and Arkansas. So, Robert, welcome.

I left our morning team meeting about 9:00 and someone told me that Rose was looking for me. That she had an ophthalmology appointment in Springdale (about 20 miles away at 10:00 and she needed a ride. I decided I could take her and by the time we got away it was nearly 9:30 and I needed to stop at Allen Canning to finalize the agreement about the delivery of ice. Remember the ice? It was almost 9:45 by the time we left Allen and there was no way we were making it to Springdale by 10:00. Hopefully, the person we asked to call that we were going to be late made the call. Never mind. No need to worry. When we reached the physician's office there was no electricity. The whole office was dark. Evidently the electrical storm during the night had done some damage to something somewhere along the line. Rose filled out her paperwork and then we decided to go to lunch. And it was one of the most enjoyable lunches I shared with someone in a long time. I think we both felt we had really gotten acquainted. We were back at about 12:30 and the lights had been on about 15 minutes. Good decision about lunch, don't you think?

Rose was reluctant to go all the way to Springdale for an eye doctor, thinking she should establish herself with an eye doctor in Siloam. We finally talked her into the appointment and I'm so glad we did. She got temporary contacts and was so elated to be able to see again. She had lost her contact supplies and extra contacts in the flooding. On the way back home she started reading the name signs in front of stores and I was forced to say, "Great, now she is going to read every sign between here and home!" She thought that was pretty funny but I had not realized how poorly she could see.

We did get the ice delivered--finally. It was one of those things where the bureaucracy takes over. Of course, none of the three managers that the Wal-Mart manager said would be available to help me get the ice loaded was available and they needed a credit card to charge to. I, of course, did not have it as the ice was donated by an individual whom I do not even know, besides, the Wal-Mart manager told me he had the number and there should be no problem in getting the ice. Ah, but there was, until a very low level manager took the chance and let us go without it. We got it there in the neck of time. I think the residents were ice-starved by the time we got it to them. Thank goodness it was a cooler day. The camp has other ice machines in the kitchen but that is only for use at mealtimes.

Here is an example of what is now happening in the camp. At 4:15 I got a call from someone saying a man needed transportation into town to pick up his daughter from daycare. He had gotten a job and he left her there for childcare while he was at work. And there is the real problem: We encourage people, especially those who want to stay in the Siloam area to get a job, but he is a single parent with a pre-school age child. What does he do with the child while he is at work? We have not provided transportation to the work site and have said that was between the worker and the employer. Neither are we providing childcare. So what is the man to do? Anyway, we got the child picked up today and he was told he would have to make other arrangements in the future. The quandary: What is the right thing to do?

Some John brown University (JBU) students sponsor a "Thursday Night Out" for 6th, 7th, 8th graders at the college and I was talking on the telephone this evening to the leader about what is needed for her to take the kids off campus and we agreed parental permission is required. I was bemoaning the fact that today is Thursday and it was really too late to get the kids informed, get permission from their parents and get them on the bus. Rose was standing there talking to another person in the group. She stepped up and said, "I'll do it, I'll be their chaperone. I'll get the permission slips and go along on the van"--of course, her own daughter is a part of that age group. You probably heard my sigh of relief all of the way to California. She is the perfect person for this role and I would never have asked her to do it. And I know I can depend on her completely.

Many activities are being turned over to the guests to do--such as some food preparation, staffing the clothing store and, of course, unloading ice. That is a healthy sign of a healthy community.

More tomorrow night about our new little dog and how she is progressing.

We are amazed and delighted about your response to helping with the adoption of Rose and her family. Rose is a singer and she had recently purchased a keyboard. That was taken by the flooding. Wouldn't that be a nice surprise if someone, or someones, wanted to give her a great gift of a new keyboard?

Rose saw the pictures of the house I described yesterday and she likes it very much. We'll see what she thinks of it when she sees it on Saturday. She had some thoughts about settling in one of the towns east of Siloam Springs that would be a little more culturally and racially diverse and have more cultural offerings. But her kids vetoed that idea right away. They are already entrenched in their new schools and want to stay here. And she feels the schools are much better than in New Orleans with smaller classes and more individual attention. So Siloam it is. Wendell and I think that if she likes the house we can have her moved in by the end of next week.

Good night,

Bettie

Friday, September 16

Day 11

Dear Friends,

It got very cold last night so today the people in charge of clothing went through the donated items looking for winter clothing. They pulled out a surprising number of coats and other heavier items but still put out a call for more donations of winter things for the rest of the day. I haven't seen the response to that call but I'm sure it will be the same as usual--too much.

The President's pledge last night to get everyone now in shelters into houses and apartments by October 15 hit a chord here at our camp. With no winterizing to be done, that date for closure does seem to be at the end of our possible life span as a shelter. By that time, although the days may still be warm, the nights will be quite cool-- possibly in the 40's.

I received a call from Project Linus today. This is an organization that makes blankets for kids. You know, Linus, the Peanuts character that always has his security blanket. The local coordinator had called me last week about bringing blankets to the kids and I kind of brushed it aside and thought we had a lot more important things to think about at that time. She called again today and with last night's temperatures I guess I was more ready to listen. This afternoon we connected with their donation of about 70 blankets and quilts for kids from infancy through high school in sizes appropriate for the age. I asked Rose and another lady in the camp to take charge of getting them to the kids. I think they will really appreciate them and I'm glad she persevered in getting to me.

All efforts are now being turned to finding out what people want to do. That has certainly been going on, of course, and our population now is just over 400, having started at about 530. But we have to intensify those efforts. This weekend a group of volunteers will canvass the camp with a questionnaire aimed at finding out people's intentions: to stay in NW Arkansas, to re-locate to another state, or perhaps they still do not know. You probably think we should have done this sooner and you would be right. But we haven't because we were too busy providing for basic needs. There seems to be lots of housing options for small families and single people but large families will be harder to place. Housing, jobs, transportation have to be coordinated--the big three--if a family unit is going to be successfully re-located here. If they are leaving here our responsibility is to see that they arrive safely at their destination and that they have indicated to us they have a place to go. We cannot restrain them here even if their plans are vague and possibly unrealistic. They are not in custody nor are they prisoners. So sometimes the packages are not wrapped in pretty ribbons, all issues completely resolved the way we would like.

I have been repeatedly told by guests to whom I have spoken, that they believe that God has given them an opportunity for a new start--a way out of the poverty in which they were entrenched. Some readily admit that had it not been for Katrina, they would never have left New Orleans even though there were better options for them in another place.

I had lunch with a man today who is here with his wife and 7 children. He left New Orleans in 1982 and settled in Pomona, CA (near LA). He returned to NO in 1984 when his mother became ill. He always wanted to leave but didn't. He had recently begun looking at several places and NW Arkansas was on his list. And here he is-- definitely not how he thought he would get here. He wants to find some land to buy and he says he needs a 5 bedroom house--he probably does but I don't know where that is going to be found. God will have to provide. He already has a job at Allen Canning and transportation is not a problem for him, to and from work, because he bought a bike with some of his money. He enjoys biking a lot, he says, but I'm not too sure how safe it is to bike on Highway 59 at midnight.

I also took a woman to the bank today. She is leaving for Louisiana tomorrow morning after her husband located her yesterday. He is in another part of Louisiana with relatives and that is where she and her son will go. She, too, has 7 children. Two are adults who have not been located. One child is with her and she has located the other four. They were evacuated by helicopter but her husband stayed behind to protect their property from looting. He finally left after the Army arrived to re-take control from the hoodlums. She has learned that her house will survive but with major work to be done in the kitchen and living room. She also has lost her little dog, Luther. She couldn't take it on the bus with her when she was taken to a shelter.

A volunteer at the station took it and told her that she would take it home with her and care for it. She cried when she told me this.

This lady was very careful with her money. She wanted to cash her FEMA check for $2,000. She needed $100.00 for spending money and then wanted some vehicle for the remainder that would be safe to transport to Louisiana. After reviewing the options she finally decided on getting a cashier's check and she plans to hide the check on her body, not in her purse where it could be snatched. A good idea. That check means a great deal to her and she is not wasting it on things like a TV or boom box. It means a start on a new life for her and her family. But she still wanted to buy my lunch with one of her five $20.00 bills.

The mother of one of our guests who is a minister died yesterday. He knew she was ill and finally made contact with other family members and learned that she had died. We are helping find transportation home for him and his family and then he wants to return to the camp after the services until he can find a new residence. There is a young woman among the citizens of the camp who is 9 months pregnant. So the circle of life continues even in the face of disaster.

Did I tell you that we named our new doggie, "Lucky Lass"? Wendell liked Lucky and I felt that was masculine. Lass is the Scottish term for young woman (girl). Chica is Spanish for little girl. So there is a connection there. Chica is extremely jealous of Lucky and tries to intimidate her frequently. Lucky is much more sedate and cool about the whole thing. Except for one teensy little problem: she has wet on my rugs 3 times today. We will take her to the vet early in the week to check on the bladder infection thing and if that is okay we just may be dealing with a stress response to all that has happened to her in the past month. But, whatever the cause, my carpets will not tolerate (nor will I) constant wetting. So we will conquer this problem--I think.

Goodnight,

Bettie

Saturday, September 17

Day 12

Dear Friends,

This is Saturday and we thought it might be a fairly quiet day, camp-wise. Not really.

The churches provide transportation to the bus station in Springdale or Fayetteville each morning for those people who are going South, East, or West by bus. It is about a 30-40 minute distance from Siloam. Part of my responsibility is to assure that there is a church scheduled to make this trip. I was uneasy about today because I had been unable to confirm with the scheduled church that they were driving. I did not know how many people would be going today but at 5:00 AM Wendell and I decided we would both go out to the camp with our car and pick-up and take the people to the bus station if the church van did not show up. And it didn't. We had six passengers and all of their belongings which are beginning to increase dramatically. We put all of the belongings in the pick-up (it is covered with a shell), a mother and her child in the pick-up with Wendell and I took four with me. It worked quite well.

Remember yesterday when I told you about the woman I took to the bank? Well, she and her son were the two who rode with Wendell. This is the first time this woman has ever been out of New Orleans and imagine the difficulty she is having in negotiating the intricacies of a long bus trip. She needed to go to this little town in mid-eastern Louisiana to meet her husband. To get there, she had to go to Houston and then to Lafayette, LA. That gets her what looks like on the map, about 3 hours from her destination. Of course, no buses go there. After talking with the agent she came out of the room in tears, not knowing what to do. We talked with the agent who was very understanding and we looked at the Louisiana map to find out where she was destined and tried to figure out something. We finally realized there was nothing to do but to get her a phone card and have her contact her husband somewhere on the trip to come get her in Lafayette. I think she is a resourceful woman but one who is totally overwhelmed by the past several weeks. If we had known about her situation earlier we could have arranged to drive her to the Louisiana destination. It is only 6-8 hours from here and I have no idea how long it will take for her to get there by bus.

We picked up Rose, Erika and Roger at noon. This was the first time we had met Erika and Roger. They are sweet kids although I'm sure Roger would not like me to say that. They are bright and funny. After lunch at Pizza Hut we went to Alltel to get a phone for Rose. We thought that was of primary importance for her (and for us when we want to contact her.) With a phone if she wishes to have potential employers contact her she has a method, if she needs to talk to her son in Baton Rouge she can. Just consider all of the times you need to use a phone or are asked for your phone number. Now think of how it would be to suddenly have to borrow someone else's phone or go to a pay phone. Not a good picture, is it?

The first call made on her phone was from Wendell and he was about 10 feet away. Just testing. The second call was from Roger to his new friend, Park, the place kicker on the football team. Park suggested they go to a movie tonight (no theatre in Siloam Springs so that means going to Springdale or Fayetteville.) Park is a good kid from a very responsible family so Rose will not need to worry about that. I'm sure she is glad to see that he is making friends quickly. Roger is a wide receiver and he will be eligible to play next Friday night. The team is 3-0 and things seem to be going pretty well so I don't know how much he will play. He will probably play quite a bit on JV.

We looked at the house that I described a few days ago and the owner told us that just this morning she had received an offer to buy the house. However, she also said that she did not intend to reduce the price so she did not know if the deal would go through. She expects to know by Wednesday. Actually, that was okay with all of us because there are rumors that the state or national government is considering paying for a year's rent for displaced persons. I talked with Dave; our City Administrator if he thought there would be any possibility of jeopardizing Rose's ability to access these funds if she left the shelter, having already obtained housing. He didn't have the answer to that, I'm not sure anyone does, but he will pursue it on Monday--of course state offices are never open on the weekend. There were some things that Rose did not like about this house anyway, although she really wants to get away from the camp. We'll continue to look for other houses. Please pray that this housing question will be quickly and positively resolved.

Then we stopped by Trinity Church where they had invited all of the people at the camp to come to a picnic on the church grounds. They also advertised that there would be free new clothes for everyone. The church's youth minister and his wife conceived the idea of kids in their church contributing one new outfit from their school wardrobe so the displaced kids could have at least one new outfit for school and to also get the church kids involved. They also planned a concert by a Christian rock band tonight for the kids. Well, of course someone decided they wanted to contribute money to this project (called Project Threads) and so the youth leaders went shopping at one of the chains (not Marshall's, but similar. Can't think of the name right now.) As these things sometimes happen the whole project gained wings and before they knew it, the store, Levi Jeans and who knows who else were contributing brand new clothing in current styles. Enough that everyone at the picnic took home a couple of outfits. Pretty great idea, don't you think?

Before we went to the church Rose insisted on buying us all ice cream at Braum's. That was important to her and many of you know how we are about ice cream so we LET her do that. Braum's ice cream is pretty good...not Dreyer's/Edy's but.....

We are hearing from many of you who now receive this letter. I have no idea how far it is being forwarded. My greetings to all of you. We appreciate those notes. You are also being generous in your support of Rose and her family. That is the important thing.

I need to close this letter as Arkansas is playing USC this evening and it is now game time. Wouldn't it be incredible if Arkansas pulled off the upset of the year? Go, Hogs, Soooooooooeeeeeyyyyyyy.

Bettie

Sunday, September 18

Day 13

Dear Friends,

Another Packers loss. How sad to watch.
Okay, now on to today's events.

Mainly, it was a quiet day. I did go to the camp and helped the Catholic priest and his crew get established for the first Catholic service. I'm not sure how many people attended but there were two there when I left about ten minutes before the beginning of the service. They brought seven or eight of their own people so if even a few more came they had a nice little group.

It is hard to ever know what the turnout for an event is going to be. We have the daily newsletter but it is apparent that not everyone reads it. But except for passing the word by mouth there is very little way to get the word around. We do have a P.A. system set up now in the dining room and that is some help but people come at various times to eat so that is not foolproof either.

A lot of the people in leadership roles at the camp also took a day or a half day off. Badly needed because several were running on empty. And next week may actually be the hardest one yet because of the necessity to beat the cold weather by getting people placed and out of the camp. It is relatively easy to feed, clothe, shelter, and provide medical care. It is even relatively easy in this area to find jobs. Housing for people who want to stay is another matter. Rental property--especially houses--are very few. And then, trying to help people who want to go elsewhere and have no contacts or family capable of taking them in, and no job is a Herculean task. Only with God's guidance will that be accomplished.

Wendell and I will look at some more housing tomorrow to see if they should be referred on to Rose. Please pray that we will be led to just the right place for her. She has a little more flexibility in rentals because of your magnificent generosity. That may make the difference in her getting into her own place in a short time.

We did name our new little dog "Lucky Lass" and she is quickly becoming just "Lucky". She doesn't respond too well to it--or anything for that matter--but she is better about the wetting on the floor--no accidents for two days. She and Chica are doing better and I even took both of them for a walk together last night, by myself. It wasn't too bad. Chica is still a tad jealous and she tries to physically get between her special people and the new dog when she can.

It was a great afternoon, just kicking back, no phone ringing, no heavy responsibility, watching the Packers game. Pretty normal, actually.

Except for the loss.

Oh, well.....

Bettie

Monday, September 19

Day 14

Dear Friends,

This was an exciting day. It started with the implementation of one of the worst ideas I have ever had. I thought it would be a good idea for me to get a firsthand look at how it is to transport volunteers from the Trinity Church staging areas to the campsite--this is about a 1/2 mile round trip. Not far apart. I thought the number of volunteers we were using had so significantly decreased that there would be no problem transporting people four at a time in our Taurus. Wrong. Really wrong. I made many, many trips to transport all of the volunteers today. We have always recruited a church van to do this job and now I have reassured myself that this is necessary. Why do I have to be a slow learner?

The full court press is on to get guests/residents placed by October 1. That is a very ambitious date, but.....it gets colder every night. So today a kind of case management approach was implemented and I think it will be more effective. A person working in this area will have full responsibility for a caseload including housing, jobs, transportation if the client wishes to stay in NW Arkansas or assisting them to re-locate wherever they wish to go. I don't believe we will be helping people find jobs in distant places but we will help to get them where they want to go.

I think it surprised some of the residents that they are expected to actively participate in the planning for their exit from the camp. That no one is going to meet every one of their needs and they are expected to leave here in a few weeks. Life has been pretty comfortable here for a certain element and I am afraid that a good many FEMA checks for $2,000 have been spent on frivolous items that have no relation to re-establishing their lives in another place until they can return home--if they want to return home. These people are the minority, but a significant minority.

And then there is Rose. We found a lovely house today and Rose is thrilled with it. It has everything she dreamed of in a new home:

3 bedrooms, 2 baths, and a well-equipped kitchen in a good neighborhood. It has a large backyard with a privacy fence. The moment Rose saw the backyard she said to Erika, "I can just see this covered with tents for an overnight party in the backyard." Already, she was thinking of ways she could use this home for the enjoyment of her kids.

Another volunteer at the camp called me this evening. She, too, is very fond of Rose and she told me that a wealthy benefactor in Springdale had given her $5,000 to pay the first month's rent for people who were staying in the NW Arkansas area and she wanted Rose to benefit from that. No problem with that! She also said that her home fellowship group was planning a shower for Rose. Another good idea! So Rose has a lot of people on her team. She will succeed. She got her Arkansas Driver's Exam manual today so now she can study for that. Wendell will take her to set up a checking account tomorrow, which will help when they go to set up the utilities for the house. I think, for some reason that eliminates the need for a deposit.

There is nothing but rumor about the proposed one year free housing for Katrina victims. I hope we don't do that. It seems to be a bit of overkill. And it would make the cost incredibly high for taxpayers. With the help they are receiving, it seems most people with the desire to work and the willingness to learn will be able to pay rent long before twelve months elapse.

Secret Service agents were all over the camp yesterday, I understand. It was in preparation for a visit by Bill Clinton. It didn't materialize, however. Cynics I talked with said it was because there weren't enough people around the Camp; it was too quiet, not enough good sound bites, to make it worth his while. I really could not comment on his motivation. Could I?

Good night.

Bettie

Tuesday, September 20

Day 15

Dear Friends,

Today is an interesting day. A day of waiting to see what the newest hurricane, Rita, will do and how it will affect us here in Arkansas. Some of our guests were ready to leave for Baton Rouge this morning but were unable to make their trip due to the uncertainty of the weather and the potential need to evacuate the Gulf--again. And, although I have not heard the news tonight there are reports of several hundred evacuees at Fort Chaffee again. I believe that is true but I need to find out where they have come from--probably the latest evacuation of the Gulf area.

All of this may upset our plans to get people settled in their new surroundings by October 1. That is an ambitious schedule anyway and this is apt to really mess up the plan. No one would be really surprised if the Arkansas Baptist Association and the Governor decided to winterize the camp and keep it open longer, taking in more evacuees. We don't want that. We want to get the people placed that we have now and close it down. But......

Every day there are fewer volunteers than the day before. Some of the leadership change daily. Those with jobs have had to resume their work life and have given as much as they can. For the most part this camp has been run by volunteers--people who have taken time off from their regular work, either because they wanted to or because their boss told them to. Meanwhile their "real" job remains undone. We knew this would happen sooner or later. I'm just glad that this can be my one and only full-time job. I have sort of become, I believe, a shoulder to cry on for other volunteers. In a highly emotional setting like this (if there are any others like this) feelings are bound to be hurt, people sometimes feel unappreciated, there is actually jealousy, and there is always someone who has a better way. Every morning our Team meetings begin with prayer and that is helpful, but Satan can ply his trade very easily here and we have to make a conscious effort to stay in control of our thoughts and to focus on what positive things are happening in the lives of these people. Remembering that it is not about us. It is about them and Him. So I try to listen, remember those communication skills that I have been taught over and over and still forget to put into practice. But I will admit that it is a little trying to have leadership changes so frequently. The people at the top--our City Administrator and the Baptist Assembly representative have stayed the same, of course, and that has given us some stability.

People are tired. People (full-time volunteers) are becoming ill at an alarming rate and I know it is the old immune system being beaten down by stress and fatigue. I feel pretty energized most of the time although once in awhile it gets to seem a lot like work rather than a privilege.

We have changed the way we recruit volunteers to carry out some of the daily tasks. We now need, besides the Leadership Team, about 50 volunteers a day. They work 4 hour shifts from 8:30 AM-7:00 PM. Now, it will be the churches' responsibility to come up with these volunteers. The Siloam churches will provide the volunteers four days/week and the churches at Springdale, Fayetteville, et al; will provide the volunteers three days a week. It has become my responsibility to assure adequate volunteers from the Siloam churches. Big job. But I have some people helping me. And I have lots of experience in staffing nursing units so this is sort of familiar except that you don't have a set number of staff to work from.

The good news today is that Rose has a job. It fits her perfectly. She was hired as a part of the small paid staff here at the camp. She will work 40 hours a week as a temporary city employee and her job will be to help connect people with jobs, housing, transportation, etc. She is perfect for that. The residents already turn to her for advice and information. They trust her and she is not shy about telling the truth even when it hurts. She starts tomorrow and will be moving to her new house over the weekend. Of course the job is temporary but it may lead to something else that is permanent with the city.

Rose and I took two other volunteers from the camp to see her house today. What a treat that was! These other two women, Vicki and Mary, have worked so hard at the camp and have seldom had the opportunity to see the fruit of their labor like they did today--Rose with a lovely new home, a new job, a new start. It was pretty special. Then we all got excited and decided how we were going to get the house furnished. Mary's daughter is an interior designer and Mary brought her into the picture and hopefully that will result in her drawing in some of her wealthy customers to give us some financial assistance in buying furniture. She will also use her skills in helping Rose with some design work. So by the time we were done today, Wendell and I were down to providing (or securing) a refrigerator and microwave. Mary and Vicki, with their contacts are taking care of the rest of the needed items! That is a good thing--giving others the opportunity to participate in this happy event. It also frees up the money that you have so generously given to help with expenses that she will incur over the next three months or so--like rent, food, etc. I'll take some pictures soon to send to you.

I think I mentioned that we were surveying residents to find out their plans. About 55 plan to stay in Siloam and about the same number hope to stay in NW Arkansas. I'm sure some in those numbers are children and this does not just reflect the head of household. Still, that is more than I expected. Our census this morning was around 375. That is a pretty significant drop.

Time for me to say good night.

Bettie

Wednesday, September 21

Day 16

(Written early Thursday, September 22)

Dear Friends,

L ast night was the first night that I didn't get my letter to you written. Fatigue, and the news I will give you below, got the best of me and when I got home at 8:00 PM, I put a dinner in the microwave and collapsed. So here is yesterday's news:

We will get 150 new evacuees today (Thursday).

Those with our current 350 or so will put us back, almost, where we started. Many of us, myself included, had to re-gear ourselves, straighten our shoulders, smile and pretend we were glad for these new guests. Of course, it won't be like it was with the first group. These people have been in shelters (usually more than one) since Katrina. Their immediate needs have been met but I am sure that many will be at the end of their emotional rope. Our job--and privilege--will be to welcome them and get them into a stable environment.

I am sure that after the Astrodome they will feel they are among the privileged to be at Arkansas Baptist Assembly. Although it is rustic, it is a lovely setting in the country. The living areas, compared to the Astrodome, are almost complete privacy--not more than 23 to a room that has 3 showers, 3 toilets, and 2 sinks.

The big deal today, this morning really, will be to get the beds made--have to find the donated bedding first. I wonder what warehouse it has been placed? Wendell retrieved 44 sheets, a bunch of pillowcases, and some pillows from the Manna Center last night so that is a start. I don't know if guests who have left the camp have taken their bedding or not. If not, we can launder that which was left and re-use them. Put that new laundry facility to work!

The Governor has come through with some actual temporary paid positions for the Camp. Really good news. So much of what needs to be done in getting people placed requires continuity and consistency. That has not been possible when relying on volunteers.

One of my continuing responsibilities is to come up with church-supplied transportation to the bus stations in Fayetteville and Springdale for people leaving the shelter. An increasing problem is the increasing amount of luggage people are taking with them. The driver of the early morning bus to Springdale yesterday told me that he had about 15 passengers on that trip--I think it is a 26 passenger people-mover. His entire luggage compartment, the five seats across the back of the bus, the aisle were all filled with luggage and people were holding duffle bags! I guess when all of your possessions have to be enclosed in a suitcase it may take more than one. Come to think of it, it took a whole van to move us from California to Arkansas. Subject closed.

I can't wait to tell Rose that my friend, Mary Lou, who receives this letter, is going to name her next dog after her. Rose will get a kick out of that. By the way, that is an honor as Mary Lou loves her doggies with great intensity.

I'm going to include part of a note that Misti sent to us after volunteering at the Camp yesterday. Thought you might appreciate it:

Bettie and Wendell,

Thank you for this incredible work going on at the camp!! I am so glad I came to volunteer today. I enjoyed it so much. I now realize and can share with the people I come in contact of the situation. I also have a great appreciation for the work of yourselves and the many volunteers that have to just not stop! I will encourage others to get involved. Please call me if you need me to work on anything for you.

Today I started working with a resident that needed help trying to reunite with her two sisters located in other areas. I will continue this work tomorrow and hopefully see it through. Another resident I interviewed made the comment that he could see the work of Jesus through all the volunteers helping here in our community! WOW isn't that our Mission? I was there just one day and you and many others are the ones working tirelessly and beautifully!

Misti

P.S. Rose is amazing, too!!!!

This, and your encouragement, and prayers, keep us going. Thank you so much.

Also, to those many of you who have sent us checks for Rose's expenses. It has been so exciting to open the mail each day. As the kids would say, "You are awesome!" Soon, we will get official thank you letters sent. But they cannot express the true way that we feel about your response. Rose will never know, unfortunately, all of you. But her new life will be a testimony to your faithfulness.

I usually say "Goodnight" here. But today, I will say, "I pray your day goes well and that you are a blessing to someone today."

Bettie

Thursday, September 22

Day 17

Dear Friends,

It wasn't 150 new people who came to populate our camp. It was 144. But not for long. One young man very early on became argumentative, almost to the point of abuse, with one of our regular (and very valuable) volunteers and was immediately placed in a patrol car and returned to Fort Chaffee. Hopefully, that will be a lesson learned by anyone else who has similar thoughts.

I was not at the camp when the new people arrived but I have heard from several sources that this group is angry. And why not. This is probably, at least for many, the third or fourth shelter they have been in. They have moved so much that their mail cannot keep up--hence FEMA checks are late in arriving, let alone contact by mail of family or anyone else. Some of the services we quickly became used to at our camp were not available to them. Medical issues are more prevalent among them than we thought they would be. Our assumption had been that because they had been in a shelter somewhere they would be at the same point in recovery that our original residents are. Wrong assumption.

You never know where a hero is going to show up. This one runs a tiny bus depot in Springdale. As I may have mentioned, every morning at 6:15 a church bus runs from the camp to either Springdale or Fayetteville to take people who are permanently leaving the camp to the bus station for the first leg of their journey home. When they get to the bus station they pick up their ticket to their destination, get on the bus and head for Fort Smith and then to wherever. Yesterday's trip included two men who were on their way to San Antonio. When they got to Fort Smith they learned that all buses going into San Antonio were cancelled because of Rita. Somehow the word was relayed back to our camp that these men were stranded. What to do. Finally someone decided to contact the Red Cross in Fort Smith to assist them. The next thing we knew that assistance had turned into bus fare back to Springdale and they were at the bus station. At 8:00 PM we were sitting at a table in Callaghan's (Siloam Springs only steak house) with

Rose and Erika when I got the call about these men being stranded in the bus station and would I find transportation to get them back to the camp. The answer to that was "No." It was too late to find someone to go, get over there (20 miles), pick them up and get home. The next thing was to figure out the alternative. My Plan B was to get them in a motel in Springdale and then get them back to the bus station to catch the bus from the camp that is there every morning at 7:00, and then ride that bus back to the camp. Are you following me? But how were we going to accomplish that? Enter Berta. She runs the bus depot at Springdale. She also runs a charter service. She found a motel, paid cash for the room (we'll reimburse her), had one of her bus drivers who had just come in from a run take them to the motel, and arranged for him to pick them up and get them back to the bus this morning for the ride back to camp. That is why she is my hero today. And this is not the only time she has stepped up when there was a need. She works diligently to get the most advantageous bus schedules for our residents--and most of the time they (the schedules) aren't really all that good. But that is not her fault. She always treats them with utmost respect and encouragement.

That isn't always the case. Rose and I were at Rose's new house yesterday waiting for Wendell and Erika before we went to dinner when one of Rose's new neighbors paid a welcoming call. Her name is Linda. When the doorbell rang, Rose was juggling two phone calls, trying to resolve a problem at the camp--remember she has been hired temporarily by the city to assist in connecting people and resolving issues--so I answered the door. I don't believe I invited Linda in. I think she came in. She didn't introduce herself until she was way inside the house. She sat down in one of the 3 plastic chairs--Rose's only furniture--and began to talk. Rose was still on the phone. Finally, she was able to get off the phone and Linda introduced herself as the neighbor across the street. Linda is probably in her 60's. About 2 sentences later she asked Rose what size she wears. Rose told her and she immediately offered her some of her hand-me-downs. Then she proceeded to tell Rose more about the neighborhood than Rose will ever want to know. She was way too solicitous, also offering her assistance in tutoring Rose's children (Who said they needed tutoring?) For free, of course. I could see Rose struggling to control herself--and doing a good job of it--but I didn't know how to get rid of this woman without being terribly rude. I gradually moved toward the door, made some comment about us needing to be on our way, and after listening to her tell us the history of the house for about 5 minutes she finally left. Rose and I just looked at each other, shook our heads and agreed that this woman was one of the world's most advanced busybodies/nosy neighbors. The purpose of her visit was clearly to find out what was going on across the street--all these black and white people were coming and going all of the time. I just wish I had introduced myself as Rose's mother. With no explanation. That would have kept her busy figuring THAT out for a long while. Later, when we related the story to Wendell and Erika it seems that Linda had come to the house earlier when they were there and told all of the same stories.

After Linda left, Rose and I were talking about the experience and Rose said that she had had several busybodies in her life--both black and white. Then she said something that I think tells a lot about her character. She said, "As a single mother people expect me to act poor--single mothers are always poor, you know. I've never had much financially, but I refuse to act poor. I act the way I was brought up and the way I want my kids to act." Right on, Rose!

Rose is determined to have her family stay in their new home tonight--with or without furniture. Their new refrigerator (that many of you helped purchase) will be delivered today. She also has a new microwave and some dishes and pots and pans. Hopefully, by the end of today she will have beds and bedroom furniture, living room furniture, a dining table and chairs--that was Mary's job to take care of and I know she will come through. Then Vicki is responsible for linens, etc.

It will be a wonderful event for them to be able to close and lock their doors tonight as a family for the first time in weeks. Their own place, their own things, arranged the way they want them. Privacy. Those things that most of us take for granted, never giving them a second thought but have been completely absent from their lives since Katrina. Oh, yes, and Rose will have a bedroom all to herself--complete with bath. In New Orleans they had a two-bedroom apartment. She gave the bedrooms to the kids and she slept on the couch. We told her that a condition of her getting this home was that she had to take the master bedroom.

Yesterday Rose told me, "I used to walk down the street, sometimes discouraged because I was just barely getting by. I would ask God to send me angels to hold me up, to help me go on. He has done that. He has surrounded me with angels who are taking care of my every need. I now have to rededicate myself to being His person and sharing the love shown to me with others."

Have a good day, Angels,

Bettie

Friday, September 23

Day 18

Dear Friends,

Remember the men I told you about on Day 17 who were stranded in Fort Smith because Rita was preventing any buses from going to Texas and the Red Cross, for some reason, sent them back to Springdale last night and we put them up in a motel for the night.

Well, the church bus brought them back to camp this morning and I ran into one of the men shortly after his return and he told me it was the best night's sleep he has had in a month. I can only imagine: A room to yourself, where you can lock the door, a thick mattress, a private bathroom. What luxuries!

It was a very quiet day at camp today given that we had registered 140+ new people yesterday. Our amazing City Administrator, Dave, who opens every team meeting now with prayer, reminded us today to have an extra measure of compassion for the people who have just joined us because they have been shuffled around so much. I didn't know until this afternoon when a truck came and dumped many, many suitcases on the Camp lawn that their belongings did not make the trip with them but came by a later bus. Many of them were like they were originally--with nothing. I think I would be angry, too.

There will be a wedding at the camp tomorrow. Watch for it on TV. This is a couple who had planned to marry around this time but their plans of course were ruined by Katrina. But when camp leadership learned of the ruined plans many people stepped in to make it a grand wedding and reception with everything from the dress to the wedding cake being donated. I won't go as I really had very little contact with the couple.

One of the deacons from our church was driving the bus tonight that picks up people and drives them here and there on the campus as some of the bunkhouses are really far from the cafeteria and where you pick up people to go to Wal-Mart. He said he was flagged down by one of our residents, a woman, who stepped on the bus, and asked, "Do you have a wife?" When he responded that he did, she muttered,

"Too bad." turned around and got off the bus. He said our orientation did not teach him how to respond when propositioned.

Rose and Erika are in their new home tonight. The furniture and linens did not make it yesterday as planned. She has a six foot folding table, 4 plastic chairs, and a mattress on the floor; the kids have pallets to sleep on, a microwave, a refrigerator, washer and dryer and a few dishes and pots and pans. But that will all change tomorrow at 4:00 when the furniture van finally comes with bedroom, living room and dining room furniture and linens. I'm definitely going to be there for that. I will take pictures. All of this was donated by people from outside our immediate area--I mean over at Springdale/Fayetteville. I think I'll take some goodies and we will have a little housewarming party before we go home. With all of this new furniture donated we will be able to help get her established with a few extras with the money you have given as well as help her with several months' rent. There is a rumor that the people who have already found housing will not share in the 12 month housing/furniture vouchers that those still in the shelters will receive. Seems this policy would encourage people to sit around and wait for the voucher before even trying to fend for themselves. I thought we rewarded people for industriousness, initiative and such. I will definitely write some letters to our representatives, the Governor and the President if Rose and others get excluded from the program because they no longer live at camp. And I think a 12 month voucher is entirely too long. Think of the price tag on these vouchers alone.

Remember Linda? I was sitting in Rose's drive today sort of waiting for Wendell to appear when I felt a tap on the window. It was Linda. She had a large floral silk arrangement for the dining table and a basket of candles. She thought they would be a nice surprise when they came in the house. Maybe we are wrong about her. You think?

Roger had an out-of-town football game tonight. This is the first game he is eligible to play and I hope he gets to actually play some. He is a wide receiver and wears that wonderful number 4. Because he went to a volleyball game last night he has never been in their new home. So he will have to find his way home tonight to a place that is completely foreign to him. I think he can handle it.

Rose was really tired tonight having lived in a whirlwind for the past few weeks. I hope she sleeps late in the morning because she has really been pushing it lately. Oh, yes, the Governor will be at the camp on Sunday morning for worship. He may bring a "special guest" with him. Anyway, Dave--our city administrator--wants to be sure that the Governor meets Rose. He'll probably be more impressed with her than she with him.

It is getting hot and dusty at the camp again but rain is on its way as a result of Rita. The days are hot and muggy and doesn't cool off much at night. But by next week the daily temperatures are only to be in the 80's--compared with our recent 90 degree days. So fall is on its way. In fact, I think it was the official beginning of fall yesterday.

Time to say goodnight,

Bettie

Saturday, September 24

Day 19

Dear Friends,

Well, the President isn't coming to the camp today so neither is the governor. Of course, we got this cancellation information yesterday (Saturday--I'm writing this early Sunday morning) only shortly after I had notified as many volunteers as possible that they were invited to the "special" worship service. I had to spend some time re-informing everyone that the worship service was still on but no longer "special." Isn't a worship service always "special"? Anyway, this is what happens, I guess, when you are dealing with politicians whose schedules change with every new event in the country. I'm not sure how many hours the Camp Director has spent dealing with the Secret Service this week as well as in previous weeks, but I know it has been many.

The wedding came off without a hitch yesterday, I am told. Even to the point of the newlyweds being driven off in a stretch limousine. I'll have to find out more of the details and let you know. I do know that the florist and caterer trucks that I saw on campus were from the very best in the area. Again, it gave people a way to provide a service to a couple and to do it in a very classy fashion.

Rose, Roger, and Erika got moved in and settled in their new home yesterday. It was pretty exciting to see that furniture van come down the street and to know it was headed for their house. By the end of the day they had new living room furniture, 3 bedrooms full of furniture, a dining table and chairs, along with linen (quite a bit of which was the wrong size and will need to be returned to Wal-Mart--but that is minor). We turned the occasion into a mini-house warming with good things to eat. A couple of JBU students were there to document the moving-in for a school project. That was fun. A neighbor from down the street--not Linda, but an old man and his little dog, neither of whose name I heard-- came and stayed a long time. Linda was there, too, and more about her later. And there were eight or so others of us who were pretty closely involved in setting up this household.

For those of you interested in this kind of thing: Erika's furniture is all white wood and she is in love with it. Unfortunately, she also fell in love with a white satin bedspread, pillows and pillow covers that had been donated--used. The only problem is that it is for a king-size bed and hers is a full-size. But she loves it even though it puddles on the floor. Her intended color for her bedding was an almost fuchsia. Rose's furniture is a dark cherry, queen size bed and is very elegant with a curved foot--almost like a sleigh bed. The bedding for it is a dark tan with burgundy pillows. Roger's room is all boy--but grown-up boy--with a dark, almost black finish to the wood with a lighter, rustic wood finish on the top of the dresser and bedside table. His bedding is a dark green plaid. The living room sofa and love seat are a brown suede and the woods are a medium oak. The dining chairs are metal with a dark wood trim and a white padded seat and the table bottom is metal with the dark wood top. All in all, everything works well together and they were tired but very pleased last night. All that is missing are the things that make a house a home but that will come from them. You have helped make that happen.

I was wrong. Roger was not eligible to play football with the team Friday night--that comes next week, but he was ecstatic about getting to travel with the team. But, they lost and are now 2-1.

About Linda, the nosy neighbor. Rose told me yesterday that she awoke feeling the Lord speak to her and telling her that she should let Linda be a blessing to her and that they, in turn, can be a blessing to Linda. So, she visited Linda yesterday morning and things started falling into place. Linda asked if Roger could possibly do some yard work for her (Linda has early Lou Gehrig's disease. She gets around pretty well with a cane.) Roger went over to her house and learned that she not only needs yard work done but is an avid football fan and has a dog. Two very large points with him. Then Rose invited her to be a part of the housewarming yesterday and she seemed to enjoy herself immensely. She did not stay a long time but she was very available to provide tools that we didn't have and anything else that was needed. Okay, okay--another lesson learned. Don't judge, don't judge, don't judge. Let God do His work and he will use each of us. Rose listened and I didn't. She is right--both of us were wrong on Thursday when we just looked at what we thought was going on with Linda. We didn't look, or realize what we could do for her. With Linda's progressive condition, over time, Rose and her family can (and will) be a great blessing to Linda. Perhaps this is why they have been brought to this place at this time. Again, I am humbled and contrite.

Rose, Erika and Roger are going to church with us this morning. Her idea, not ours, as we want the family to attend wherever they feel most comfortable. But we are glad they will be with us today. There are so many who are eager to meet them.

Today, Sunday, will be a day off for us--really a day off. I don't think I told you about the Seventh Day Adventists--maybe I did but I will tell you about it again. They offered to provide all of the volunteers, transportation for volunteers, and their orientation on Sundays. That allows all of those who worship on Sunday to have that day free. What a blessing they are to all of us!

I'll write about Day 20--Sunday--tonight.

Bettie

Sunday, September 25

(Written early September 26)

Day 20

Dear Friends,

Yesterday was Sunday, Day 20. It was almost a day off. I didn't go to camp but I did field telephone messages and respond to Katrina related e-mails. All in all I expected it to be a more restful day than it was. And on top of it all the Packers are now 0-3.

And we won't even think about what happened to the Razorbacks on Saturday.

Rose, Roger and Erika went to church with us yesterday and the two kids instantly disappeared with friends they had made at school who attend church at Community Christian. Rose loved the music and the sermon and the friendliness of the people. She told us afterward that she thought she had found her church. We would like that very much but we have been reluctant to encourage her toward CCF because we don't want her to feel that she has to go to our church out of obligation to us.

I've been meaning to tell you about S.I.F.E. You may have heard about it. It is a college-level organization for students in business and the letters stand for "Students in Free Enterprise." One of their student leaders at JBU (John Brown University here in town) contacted me last week and said they wanted to give free bikes to three of the kids at the camp. Sounded like a good idea to me. She said they frequently do a program in which groups of their members are given the materials to make a bike. They are told that this is a contest and they naturally believe the first team done is the winner and they speedily put together the bike--speed being the operative word here. At the end of the exercise they bring out the three chosen kids and introduce them as the students' customers. The lesson they are to learn from this is that the bike-makers had no idea of who their customers were and what their needs were. They were only thinking of themselves and winning the "contest." And, in order to make a successful product you need to know your customers. Interesting concept. Maybe real companies should adopt that approach. So at the end of the whole thing the three kids get to take home a new bike and a helmet--not the bike put together by the students.

My job was to find the three kids. Not as easy as you might think, but I called on my main resource for what is happening at the camp--Rose--and asked her for the names of three kids between 8-11 who should be considered. She told me about Dennis who is 9 years old. I went to see him and his Mom to gain her permission. She seemed rather spacey when I talked with her and I wasn't sure I was getting through to her. I later learned she had verbally attacked Rose at the beginning of the camp but that had been resolved. For some reason Dennis does not go to school. Some parents made that decision because they did not think they would be here that long. But here we are at Day 20 and Dennis is just hanging around all day.

The second kid is 10 year old John. I talked with his grandmother on Saturday and learned she is his guardian. She paid attention to my story and was eager for John to be included. John, of course, was ecstatic. I mentioned that I needed to find a third student and John's grandmother instantly said, "My niece, she is the right age." She went inside and called her sister, Oschelle's grandmother, who is also her legal guardian. Her name was Lynn and she, too, thought this was a great idea and Oschelle was dancing for joy. Lynn pretty much took charge then saying where the kids should meet their ride to take them to JBU after school and that she personally would meet the bus driver on Tuesday morning to let him know that the kids would not be riding the bus on Tuesday evening. None of this group knows Dennis and just shook their heads about him not being in school.

Can it be this easy to arrange? I've learned that most things regarding the camp are not that easy. Communication is still mostly face-to-face. People are hard to find in their bunkhouse. You go to a room that is designated on our records as the home of an individual and you find they have moved to another bunkhouse but no one knows where. So then the search is on. If you're lucky you only spend a short time before you can track them down but it is not unusual to spend an hour or two delivering a message.

We took a picture of Lucky Lass this morning. She is in bad need of a trip to the groomer. But we wanted to catch a photo of her before she got all purtied up--just as she came to us. She is a very sweet little dog but we are still having some piddling problems. What to do. We have never trained a dog. Chica came to us perfectly trained. Is this an adjustment thing? Are we not spending enough time with her?

We would like to take a picture of her and Chica together but they don't hang out together much. We're working on that.

Enjoy your day,

Bettie

Monday, September 26

Day 21

Dear Friends,

For those of you who questioned Lucky Lass' lack of hairstyle you will be glad to know she has an appointment on Friday for a total 'do. She is also going to the vet tomorrow afternoon for her complete check-up.

Today was an interesting exercise in a little camp frustration. Part of my role has evolved into providing transportation. A lot of this is being done by churches so I guess that is where I came in. Anyway, I knew at the end of last week that a family was moving today to the Spring Valley Apartments here in Siloam. I took our pick-up to the camp this AM with the intention of using it to help move them and Wendell was standing by as back-up to help load things if it were necessary. At 9:00 this AM I went to their room to let them know I was there to help move them and other roommates said they had moved out this weekend. Of course, there was no record of them actually leaving. The procedure is that when someone leaves permanently they complete exit papers with their forwarding address. Also, at that time they cease to be eligible for camp benefits (like medical care) and are then on their own in dealing with FEMA and any other governmental entity. I suspect this family just had the opportunity to leave this weekend and took it rather than wait until today.

Then the second incident was a little like the first. I was in the camp office and a lady came up because she wanted a ride to the Fayetteville Holiday Inn Express. She had seen an ad for a job there--I believe in housekeeping. I arranged to meet her at the gazebo at 1:30 and I would drive her there. 1:30 came and went and I went to her room and could not find her. I hung around until 2:00 with no sign of her. Who knows what happened. But that wastes a lot of my time. She will probably show up tomorrow wanting a trip to Fayetteville to apply for a job. And we will see that she gets there but I admit my enthusiasm for getting her there has dimmed.

Then there was the phone call from a volunteer who received a call (how this happened, I will never know) from one of our families-- parents and 5 children--who has been staying in the Best Western in West Siloam Springs. Well, for those of you who are geographically challenged, West Siloam is adjacent to Siloam but it is in Oklahoma. Some families have been housed, for various reasons, not at the camp but at local hotels--paid for, I believe, by the Red Cross. I'm not sure why this family was at the Best Western. Anyway, they called because they thought they had arranged to take their children for school registration today but no one had showed up to take them. I called the Siloam Superintendent of Schools, and just as I thought, he cannot pick up kids in Oklahoma even if they theoretically are a part of our Arkansas Camp. If they want to put their kids in school they will have to move to an Arkansas hotel or back to the camp, or enroll them in the Concord, Oklahoma, school district and I don't think that was their intent. Like a good manager, I promptly shuffled that whole problem off to someone else because it definitely is not within my scope of responsibilities. I'm learning to do that--not try to solve all of the problems. Frequently, I don't have all of the right answers and I could mess it up for everyone.

This living in motels has created a lot of problems. The people may not have transportation. They probably have to provide their own food. They are outside the stream of communication and may not be at camp when services come on campus that they may need.

The other problem that is developing because of our proximity to Oklahoma is the Cherokee Casino. It, too, is in West Siloam Springs. It seems our residents have discovered the casino and some are visiting it regularly. Of course, we have no control over how they spend their money. We just don't transport them there. That is also where they get their alcoholic beverages. Did I tell you that our county (Benton) is a dry county? And Siloam is even dryer. In most of Benton County "private clubs" can sell alcohol. And to become a member of the club you usually just have to sign a guest book (sometimes not even that.) Siloam doesn't even allow that. Not so in Oklahoma where the first business you see is a liquor store and the second is the casino.

Then the good story of the day. There is a man who since about the first day he arrived with the first group has volunteered in the dining room, washing dishes and doing whatever he could. I had seen him a lot but had never talked to him before. Today I was sitting in my "office"--you may remember that is the front porch of a cottage a little off the beaten path where it is a quiet place to think and return calls. He came up and asked a question about how to get his immunizations and he told me that he is heading to Wichita next week where he has relatives. He is retired from the armed services where he served as an LPN. Since that time he has worked part-time in nursing homes, but mostly has done volunteer work. With his retirement from the service he has sufficient income, he says, to allow him to do this. When the Governor was here a couple of weeks ago he purchased a bouquet to give to the First Lady. Through some mix-up he was in Fayetteville when the Governor and First Lady were here so someone else presented her with his flowers. She gave that person her card and said she would like to talk to the person who gave her the flowers. So he called her the next day and much to his surprise, she immediately came on the line and they had a very enjoyable conversation. At the end he told her that if her husband ever runs for President she should be his spokesperson. She evidently thought that was pretty funny. The really funny thing is that that will very likely happen. Governor Huckabee is now Chair of the Governor's group and gets quite a lot of press. He is known to be ambitious and he has been very upfront and involved in the hurricane relief effort. We could find a lot worse candidate. But is the country ready for another President from Arkansas? This one is different. He is a Baptist minister and a Republican. And he and his wife recently entered into a covenant marriage--a little mechanism in Arkansas that makes it harder to get a divorce, although I don't remember all of the details. It is supposed to encourage people to stay married and also signals others that you have a strong marriage. Hmmmm...

Lots of little loose ends to tie up tomorrow. Why don't those things take care of themselves?

Good night.

Bettie

Tuesday, September 27

(Written Wednesday, September 28)
Day 22

Dear Friends,

Yesterday morning--Day 22--David began the session by saying, "What day is this?" I quickly spoke up and said, "Day 22", since, as you know, I've been keeping track. Of course, for those who have been a part of the planning process before the evacuees came, it has been about 3 days longer. In the beginning David always wrote the day on the white board at the front of the room but that has long passed and now it is just another day at the Camp--trying to re-locate people and re-unite families.

We got a summary last night of where the remaining 276 family units are: 43 want to remain is Siloam, 46 want to go to the I-540 corridor, 38 want to stay in NW Arkansas but have no preference as to where. 49 want to go back to New Orleans--many of these are older people, 27 are waiting of FEMA, SS checks, etc., but know where they want to go. 24 are ready to go but have had travel interrupted by Rita. 49 are undecided. A large number of the last group was among the arrivals last Thursday. I find it very interesting that so many want to remain here. I am sure those are the ones who see the opportunities in available jobs--something that most say was not possible in New Orleans. Toward the end of the week, those who have not made any move toward planning for the future will be transported back to Fort Chaffee where they will have winterized quarters and will allow the team here to concentrate on helping those people who have shown that they want to get on with their lives. At first glance, that sounds a little cruel, but it isn't. It is the right thing to do for both groups. Those who are just living off the fruit of the land, so to speak, are also those who tend to cause trouble and that is certainly not in the best interest of the camp. They take time and focus away from those who are trying to get out of our facility. And it is getting cold. If they intend to spend the winter in a shelter it might as well start now in one that is winterized. As David often says, "Don't mistake our meekness for weakness."

Judy, David's assistant, and I were visiting yesterday morning before our 8:00 meeting and we discovered that of the 8-10 people in the room at the time she and I were the only ones who were there the first day. Of course, David, the chief of police, and the city's financial person came in later and they were definitely there on that day. But it just shows how the faces have changed over time. Many of those who helped get us through those crucial first days have gone back to their lives. The First Baptist Church of Springdale has a much lower profile and the churches of Siloam have a much higher one. FBCS knew how to respond to the crisis and had the resources to do it, but it is the churches of Siloam that are here for the long run.

Wendell has gone to the camp this morning to help transport luggage to the bus depot in Springdale. The luggage belongs to the 20 people or so who are leaving the camp this AM for a lot of places-- primarily south. Getting the luggage there has become more of a problem than getting the people there. The bus holds about 26 and has a luggage compartment but there is so much baggage that, without another truck carrying part of it there is not enough room for everything. I understand the bus companies have relaxed their rules about the amount of luggage people can bring on board so that evacuees can carry their possessions with them. Nice idea and compassionate. I'm not sure how long they can continue to do that. Another one of those things nobody thought about and a detail you would never think about until you have lived through it.

Enjoy your day,

Bettie

Wednesday, September 28

Day 23

Dear Friends,

This was a very hectic day. As I wrote this morning Wendell went to camp at 6:15 AM to help transport luggage belonging to the 20+ people who were taking the bus at Springdale as the first leg of their trip to a new life. And now for the rest of the story: The luggage filled Wendell's pick-up and every spare spot in the bus and a 15 passenger van that also went along. I later talked to the woman who runs the bus station at Springdale and she said her husband had to use one of their charter vehicles to take the luggage that could not make it on the bus to Fort Smith!

I brought up the problem at staff meeting this morning and offered some options. The first option, and the simplest, would be to limit each person to two bags. However, in light of their having lost close to everything in the Hurricane and flood, most of the Team was reluctant to do that. The second was to limit the number of evacuees departing to a number where our bus could hold both the people and their things. With our mission to get everyone relocated by October 15, that seemed counter-productive. So we opted for the third idea. We decided to rent a small moving van from Ryder to carry their luggage! Amazing for people who arrived with nothing.

Then I made a big mistake. About 11:00 I was told that we only have 4 people going out on the bus Thursday morning. I called the City Administrator's assistant who was handling the truck rental and told her that we would not need it until Friday. Huge mistake. By 2:30 that number had risen to 26. And us with no truck. By the time I got that message, it was too late to re-engage the truck for tomorrow. Not knowing what else to do, I called the City Administrator (Dave) and told him about the problem and he quickly said, "No, problem. I'm with the guy now who can make another truck happen." He must have meant Art, the Siloam Public Works guy. So tomorrow morning we will not have a Ryder truck. We'll have a City of Siloam Springs truck hauling luggage.

I didn't get to see the kids today who got the new bikes yesterday evening. I'm looking forward to their stories.

Then the big event of the day. It rained very hard this afternoon so when Wendell came home he found Lucky, who was outdoors in the rain, hiding under some bushes. He brought her in the house dried her off, fixed her house in the garage, put a leash on her, gave her food and water and left her there. When I came home I drove into the garage, saw her there, took pity on her and decided to bring her into the house. Another mistake: I took the leash off in the garage. She bolted out the open garage door before I had even realized what had happened. I chased her across our 2 acres, past two neighbors, across the field of another neighbor and down into the "hollow." All in all, it was at least a half mile. And I RAN after her almost all of the way. I didn't know I could do that. What finally stopped her at the 4th house she came to were three ceramic animals: a pig, a cat, and a dog sitting by the doorstep. Those caught her attention and she stopped to inspect them. When I realized that I was not going to easily catch her, I had pulled my cell phone out of my jeans pocket and frantically called Wendell who was in the house at home. I don't know if he really understood my call or not. I thought he would get in the pick-up and speed down and help me catch her. Instead, he too, ran all of the way. By the time he caught up with us I had caught her and then all three of us had to walk back home.

We had a few bad minutes this morning in our meeting when we learned that someone from another Arkansas shelter was testifying before Congress today about how they had run a model shelter for Katrina evacuees. We kind of moaned because they had tried to tell us how to run our camp and were kindly told to not come back. Their camp held 52 hand-picked evacuees, taking only those who could demonstrate their willingness to re-locate and work. Rose, probably the only Christian in the room at that moment, was quick to say that they have their reward. Ours may come later but it will be the one that counts.

Good night.

Bettie

Thursday, September 29

Day 24

Dear Friends,

Our big news of the day was the weather. We had rain yesterday afternoon and then a cold front came through and it was in the 40's at camp this morning. Very, very brisk and sunny. Thank goodness for the sun because I think we did hit the 70's by mid-day. And it is supposed to get even a few degrees cooler tonight. People were in a surprisingly good mood this morning. Maybe they were just glad to have survived the night! We have given out so many blankets and all of the winter clothing that we can lay our hands on. I am sure that the weather will make returning to Fort Chaffee much more palatable to those who have to go back there tomorrow and next week. Those are the people who actually have made no plans. There were about 30 who were to have been relocated back there tomorrow but that number was reduced by 11 late today.

The reason 11 people will not be going to Fort Chaffee tomorrow is because one of them was hospitalized today. This is an extended family. I'm not sure who all is in the group but I know there are 4 kids who belong to Tina, there is Tina and there is her mother. Tina is 35 and 33 weeks pregnant and one of our volunteers took her to see the obstetrician today and they found protein in her urine and slightly elevated blood pressure so she was hospitalized for some more testing and to determine whether to induce labor. So the whole family will remain at the camp until it is determined what will be Tina's outcome. There may be a family of 12 who ultimately go to Fort Chaffee.

It is troubling to think of a family this size with a newborn living in an army barracks. But it could be worse--it is both heated and air conditioned, they will live together in a barracks setting, they will have warm meals, medical care, the kids can be enrolled in school. It is much better than it will be at our camp in a couple of weeks. But is that the best alternative for them? We cannot force them to go anywhere. They are being offered Fort Chaffee. They have not been able to make any plans for themselves to get out of their current situation. There are no plans for getting a job. We can only go so far in what we do for them. Personally, I believe the government--state and federal--has been very generous to the hurricane victims. Add to that the extreme generosity of private individuals, organizations and churches and you have an enormous outpouring of resources. Some, probably most, are using this experience to rebuild their lives, as the money was intended. Too many are using it, probably like they have always used money given to them, in a senseless, extravagant shopping and gambling spree. And when it is gone, then what?

A reunion is happening tomorrow. A young, developmentally disabled man and his legal guardian, Gilda, will be reunited at the Northwest Arkansas Regional Airport tomorrow night. Lionel, the young man, was finally found in a Red Cross shelter in Jacksonville, Florida. I am sure he has been a difficult resident to take care of. Evidently he wanders a lot. Fortunately, he was "adopted" by a volunteer worker who has built a relationship with him. She raised the money for his $500.00 flight expense to Arkansas tomorrow. Gilda, too, is a fine woman. Lionel is not a relative but she has always been close to him and has become his legal guardian. They will stay here together for a few days then, hopefully, leave together for Houston.

The continuing saga of Lucky. I took her to the vet today after having to cancel her appointment early in the week. When we got to the exam room she quickly squatted and urinated--blood-very bloody. Well, at least we know that she still has a bladder infection and there was enough urine that the vet collected it for a urinalysis. Come to find out the medication that she had been on for the infection was much too low a dose (according to the manufacturer's recommended dosage) to be effective. Now it had progressed to this point. This was the first time that we had observed the very grossly bloody urine. I'm glad it happened at the vet's office. There were no crystals in the urine to indicate she has bladder stones. Now she is on an appropriate dosage of a different drug for 3 weeks. Hopefully that will take care of it. She is also overweight (she weighs 23 pounds) so she was put on a Hill's Science diet that is for weight reduction and acidifies the urine. And we still have to get her shots when this is all over. We may have to ask you for assistance in paying her vet bills! Just kidding (I hope.) But she is a sweet dog and she does not act like she is ill. I can't wait to see her tomorrow after she has her hair done.

Our camp count this morning was 357. Notice how much more we are focusing on numbers? Another number is 16. That is the number of days till the camp closes. It is coming soon.

Good night,

Bettie

Friday, September 30

(Written Saturday, October 1)
Day 25

Dear Friends,

I know, I know, it is Saturday morning and you have not yet received Friday's chapter. We went to the Siloam Springs High School football game last night and got home rather late (10:30) so I decided to write this morning. Siloam won, by the way, 14-6. They are now 3-1 which is better than some professional teams I could cite. Rose and Erika went with us. Roger suited up but did not get in the game. I think that was something of a relief for Rose. She is much more enthusiastic about his interest in basketball than she is his interest in football. He is tall and skinny with long legs. Even a high school linebacker could squash him in a minute.

I am observing an interesting phenomenon that has always been present but one to which I have not been sensitive. It happened again at the game last night. As African Americans Rose and her family stand out wherever they go in this pretty-much Caucasian community. I'm sure there are more Hispanics here than African Americans. And Siloam is a small town--12,000 max. So, as in all small towns news travels fast. Might as well have put Rose's picture on the front page. She has become a celebrity. She handles that much better than I would, I'm sure. At the game last night, people I am sure she has never met treated her like an old friend. She and the woman sitting next to her laughed and talked throughout much of the game--pals. And after the game as we were walking to the car Roger's English teacher stopped her. Now how did she know Rose was Roger's Mom? Anyway, the teacher proceeded to do a Parent-Teacher Conference right there. All good, by the way. She told Rose how well Roger is doing and how he wants the lead in all of the plays they are reading in class. I can see that in Roger.

I have mentioned before that a lot of camp families want to stay in NW Arkansas primarily because of the availability of jobs and the desire for a new start in life. Many felt hopeless in New Orleans. Siloam has an abundance of jobs but all of the available housing is gone. Last week our crack relocation team went to work. This is a group of people who started out as volunteers but have been put on the City's temporary payroll to do this very important job at the camp and to provide consistency and who have developed expertise in getting people connected with housing. They realized that there was a 3-pronged approach that needed to be developed: housing, jobs, transportation. After consultation they decided that the first part to attack was housing. But the problem was getting people to the I-540 corridor cities to look at housing (20-30 miles east of Siloam). I should back up this just a bit and be sure you realize what this Governor has done. He has promised the evacuees who settle in Arkansas will receive rent and utilities assistance for 12 months plus financial assistance in obtaining furnishings for their apartment/house. Wow! Hopefully, Rose will share in this as well. Starting yesterday the camp has buses that will run 2 times a day to 3 different areas in the I-540 corridor so people will be able to look at housing. They will be given a list of 3 available places to look at and then will be asked to make a choice and hopefully come back to the camp with a signed lease. This will allow them to get into housing immediately, the furniture will be obtained from a large local furniture store and they will leave the camp within a few days. Then when they are living in the area they will be able to look for a job and will probably have no trouble finding one--that is the environment here. Some have already located jobs but getting from the camp to the job has been a problem. This team put together an awesome plan and it is working.

Our census was 342 yesterday morning and a few have left since then. Plus the 27 we sent back to Fort Chaffee yesterday because they have no plans except to return to New Orleans and New Orleans is not ready to return to.

Our camp is gearing down in most ways except for what I described above. People have fallen into a routine. Mail comes in the morning. Always an interesting time with long lines of people waiting for FEMA checks or word from home. Children go off to school. Others go off to dental, medical or eye appointments. They do the laundry, straighten their living areas. Volunteers are there to assist where they can but the overwhelming numbers of questions and issues of the first two weeks have been resolved and life is pretty quiet. Now and then someone decides to confront another and there has been an occasional arrest. All-in-all, though, it has been mercifully crime and bad behavior free. Thank God for that and it has never been the tinder box the police chief warned us of. That may be because of the strong police presence 24 hours a day.

I'm gearing down as well. Wendell and I will be leaving next week for a long-planned vacation to a wedding in Indianapolis, then on up to Milwaukee and Green Bay for a few days. My last day at the camp will be next Tuesday. I wish I could be there when the lock is closed on the front gate of the camp and the work is over but that won't happen and we will learn about that last 10 days from others' stories. October 15 is still the last day.

Have a wonderful day.

Bettie

Saturday, October 1 and Sunday, October 2

Days 26 and 27

Dear Friends,

I just realized that I will be back for the closing of the camp! We will be back from vacation on the 13th and I'm sure they will let me show up on the 14th and/or the 15th. Makes me feel a lot better. That is the truth. I really want to be there when it is over.

This is the weekend and it has been so quiet that my cell phone only had one voice mail on it this afternoon--from the whole weekend. Did I tell you about our cell phones? We were Verizon customers in California and were very satisfied with the service and the plan we were on. When we moved to Arkansas we learned that Verizon does not operate here and we would have to switch companies. We decided to stay with Verizon. This meant that our cell area code is 562. That was really not a big problem because my cell phone was used mainly to call Wendell on his phone or to call home or to call long distance as we do not have long distance service on our land line. We also had lots and lots of minutes on our cell that we never used. Until now. Over the past month we have racked up the minutes on this line. And between our two lines the total is 4500 minutes--3500 of those in peak time. 2500 of them are on my line. I don't even know how many minutes our plan allows us but I know we have never, ever, come close to using this amount. I'm not whining about the minutes. I'm really telling you this to help you see how important the cell phone has been in our camp communication system. My cell phone minutes have been only a small part of the usage when you put together the total cell phone minutes of the entire Team. I hope all of the people who called our 562 number had nationwide service.

I wanted to tell you about some of the unsung heroes of this camp. There is Jim who for the past 2+ weeks has been at the camp 6 days a week with the 24 passenger church bus to transport people from the camp to the Springdale bus station. He has been there every day and sometimes twice a day in order to take people to the 6:00 PM bus. I sometimes hesitate to call him because he never refuses. Actually,

I always want to call him because he never refuses. What a quandary! Jim works in the Wal-Mart corporate offices in Bentonville and I think he is involved in opening new stores. He is a deacon at our church and is in charge of the Transportation Ministry. He has put over 1000 miles on the bus and van going back and forth to the bus station. This morning at church he said we should figure out a way to go to the apartments where people have moved and be there to bring them to church if they want to come. Interestingly, our church administrator says that since he has been involved with the camp he has been more attentive to his responsibilities with the vehicles at church. He also told me that the bus has been running better than it has in a long time due to the increased usage. Is that sort of like us? Do we "run" better when we are used more? When we are busy doing work that we know is worthwhile? Just a thought.

There is Scott who is the Camp Manager. That is his full-time job and he and his family live at the camp. He never comes to our leadership meetings but he is the go-to guy for anything that doesn't work right, he sees that trash is picked up, that the lights work, that food is ordered, that ice is on hand. All of those things that you don't notice until they don't work. Without him we would be in a terrible situation.

David, the City Administrator, came to our house yesterday morning to pick up some money. I have become the person who knows where the money is that has been donated to churches. It seems when some churches don't know what to do with disaster money that has been collected they call me. I usually tell them to hold on to it and I will call them when there is a need.

Well, David called Friday and said he needed $250.00 to give to a family who was leaving in their own vehicle but did not have travel money. I got the money and on Saturday David came to get it. He stayed for about an hour and we found out a lot about him. He used to be a youth minister in the inner city of St. Louis. He said he, his wife, and kids were probably the only Caucasians living in an 8 block area. So when a black minister from Fayetteville, dressed in suit, tie and a beautiful watch, got in his face recently and repeatedly told Dave that "you can't possibly understand the culture," David told him to go to the internet, look him up and find out why what he was saying was not true. The minister really wanted to come in and run the camp. I think I told you that Dave opens each Team meeting with prayer. You can tell he is no stranger to having conversations with God. But Rose describes what Dave does at those meetings better than I. She says he "holds a Bible study every morning." And she is right. He can, it seems for every situation, pull out of his Biblical knowledge, a scripture that pertains to the situation and describes our dilemma, issue, victory, exactly the way we need to view it. He is a very special man for this very special time.

Our friend Bette, with whom I used to work in California, drew our attention to the September 30 edition of *Newsweek* where there is an article called "The Dispossessed" and one of our residents, Glenda Smith, was interviewed. Wendell went to USA Drug yesterday to get the magazine but the latest one he found was dated September 26. Takes a while to get to Arkansas, I guess. So I looked up the article on *Newsweek's* website. Bette is right. Glenda is not a happy person. She and her family are a part of the 144 who came a week or so ago from Houston. They have been moved around a lot and now, because they want to return to New Orleans and that is not yet possible, they will be sent back to Fort Chaffee when our camp closes. She says the camp is "like a prison." Some prison. I don't know one where you are free to come and go as you like, one that offers free bus rides to town and Wal-Mart every hour during the daytime, free health care (I guess a prison does that). She is right when she says the camp does not serve red beans and rice and I guess if you are looking for a little bit of home that could be important. But in the whole scheme of things, is it really? As the article says, "Smith is mad at just about everything." I don't know how soon after arriving at the camp Ms. Smith was interviewed. But she sounds like a woman who has been stretched to her limit and needs several good nights of rest. She says she hasn't received her FEMA check. That limits her options if she has no other resources. I don't know when she applied for it. I do know that many people at the camp have received FEMA checks and for the most part received them very promptly. Perhaps it is having a hard time catching up with her since she has moved frequently.

The article also quotes a Celery Hudson, apparently from our camp, who says he is told he is "not in the computer." So he can't get his FEMA check or other benefits. I just looked him up on our roster and he isn't there, either. Some people have given more than one name and that only complicates the problem. I don't know if that is the case with him or not, but it could be.

The article also gives examples of people doing silly things "because there is nothing else to do." That really is true to a certain extent. Kids are in school but adults are not being entertained nor given classes on-site for anything. I do know some have discovered the local public library. A few have found temporary jobs. Most are spending an incredible amount of time trying to put their lives back together. But there are those who simply are waiting to see what happens next and who will help them. And time, for them, hangs heavy. But the camp's purpose was never to provide long-term rehabilitation. It is to provide shelter, clothing, food, needed medical care and relocation services as well as reuniting families.

I've spent a lot of time writing about this article, haven't I? I guess my frustration is coming through, too. We have worked very hard at making the camp work and want people to recognize this and be appreciative. We want a pat on the back. We want to be told we have done a good job. And now there are people who feel we have not done enough. Is that true? Should we have done more? Perhaps. Why didn't *Newsweek* interview Rose or one of the other families who has been successful in re-locating and leaving the camp? Why don't I just leave the whole thing to God?

Good night.

Bettie

Monday, October 3

Day 28

Dear Friends,

It is halftime, Packers vs. North Carolina, and my brother, Leon, just sent an e-mail saying that unless I like Tim McGraw (the halftime performer) I should just go to bed and get an extra hour of sleep. I appreciate his concern for my welfare but I think I will just stick it out with all the rest of you Packers fans. It hasn't been, however, an inspiring first half--to say the least.

Newsweek **did** interview Rose at the same time that they interviewed Glenda. I guess they were looking for a particular slant for their story. Perhaps I don't understand journalism. Perhaps I naively thought that journalists did interviews and wrote articles based on the interview--not that they interviewed until they found a subject whose opinions supported their own. Including Rose's experience would have at least provided a balanced and much more realistic viewpoint.

Today I spent most of my day taxi-ing people from place to place. It was really kind of fun because it gave me a chance to talk with people more than usual. I talked with 3 ecstatic families who have found housing in the area and will be moving in the next few days. One, Nathan, whom I think I told you about several days ago--the retired army LPN who planned to go to Kansas to be near his brother--has found an apartment in Fayetteville. He said he could not pass up the 12 months free housing. It will give him an opportunity to decide what he wants to do next.

Another is a family of six--parents and 4 kids--who today found a house in Siloam Springs that has three bedrooms and they are so happy with it. The wife said the first thing she is buying when she gets in the house is a juicer. She told me she had been diagnosed with "beginning cancer" and she started drinking juices--veggie and fruit--and she feels so much better and believes she is cured. She has not seen a physician, however, to confirm this.

Then there is the couple that I took across the state line to the casino tonight so they can celebrate the finding of their new apartment in Springdale. They really weren't going there to gamble but to have the casino's po' boys sandwich. I've never eaten at the casino but it could be the best food in town. That would not be difficult.

And there were the two older ladies I took to the bank so they could cash a check and have some money before they leave tomorrow for Baton Rouge. They have been friends a long time, having lived in the same building in New Orleans. They are going to a shelter in Baton Rouge with the idea of then getting home to New Orleans when it opens up. More of the older people want to go back to New Orleans than those who are younger.

Our census is now under 300 and we fully expect it to drop dramatically over the next few days. The possible hold-up now is the inspection of each new residence by HUD. Without the HUD okay the 12 month payment of rent will not happen. However, the local HUD office said it's one inspector can inspect 15-20 units a day if there is not much travel between units--like in one large apartment complex. That is a pretty quick inspection, seems to me. Especially when she says the inspection is a 12 page document.

One of our guests is schizophrenic (probably more than one) but this one became particularly distraught over the weekend and had to be taken to the ER. He was given medication there and then today he had a prescription to be filled and I said I would run to Wal-Mart and have it filled (a nursey thing to do, wouldn't you say?) Patrick, who always seems to have a wad of bills from some government pot to use for stuff like this, gave me a $100.00 bill to pay for it. When I went to pick up the Rx the cost was $195.00 for a 30 day supply. Wow! We found out later we probably could have billed this to Medicaid as they have waived some of their rules for Katrina. But we didn't know that at the time. He will probably have to be placed in an inpatient facility here in NW Arkansas for awhile before he rejoins his family. It sounds as though the family would prefer that. Incidentally, Wal-Mart stopped giving out free medication to the evacuees on October 1. I can't blame them. They have done a great deal more than one could ever expect from a large corporation.

The Paul Taylor dancers are performing this week at the Walton Fine Arts Center in Fayetteville. A part of their troupe is performing tonight at the Siloam Springs High School. They gave an unlimited number of free tickets to the camp and we sent a van and a car full of people there this evening. It should have been a very enjoyable adventure.

Time to go and hope for a better second half.

Good night,

Bettie

Tuesday, October 4

Day 29

Dear Friends,

Zack is missing. Zack is a beautiful black lab, who with his good friend, Pax, is a big part of the camp, belonging to Scott, the camp's permanent manager. Their names, by the way, are short for "Prozac" and "Paxil", probably because they are a good alternative to taking an antidepressant drug. Many days as I drove on to the campus I could depend on both of them lying smack dab in front of me on the lane leading down into the camp, not moving until the last moment, and always behaving like a well-prepared welcoming committee. Everyone around the camp knows the dogs. Now Zack has not been seen since Sunday. There is no way that he would run off. The sinister fear is that he has been kidnapped and there are two theories. The first is that a resident, or residents, loaded him into their vehicle as they permanently left the camp (he probably would not have resisted) or the second theory--even more sadly--is that he was removed by a disgruntled volunteer as she left. This volunteer, a young woman, had been reprimanded on more than one occasion on Sunday for inappropriate behavior with a young male resident and had ultimately been told to leave and not return. $100.00 award posters with Zack's pictures were put up all over the camp yesterday. What a sad thing to happen here at the end of the whole evacuee experience.

Our census is now around 200. I say "around" because no one really knows. You're wondering, I'm sure, how that can possibly be. Well, if can be possible because people are free to leave when they want. Contrary to what you may read it is not a prison. In the beginning, people were asked to sign out with Security every time they temporarily left the campgrounds. That became ineffective pretty quickly as people came and went several times a day. People are still asked to go through an exit procedure when they leave permanently. And most do but there is no legal requirement. There are some people still on the roster who have not been seen in weeks. They are probably self-sufficient people who, early on, made arrangements for relocation and just left the camp on their own.

Day before yesterday a house-to-house census was begun and is still only partially finished. It is revealing that we have a few people on the roster who are listed twice--two different names--and several that no other residents know. I am sure that when the gates are closed a week from Saturday (those are symbolic gates, by the way, as there are no actual gates to the camp) our records will show there are several people for whom we cannot account. Makes one wonder about all of the other shelters in the country and the numbers of people that are reported in those shelters.

The Closing-Down Strategy is in full force now. When I look back over the activity of the first weeks compared to now there are so many changes to the services and all of it sends a message to the residents that their days at the Arkansas Baptist Assembly are coming down to a precious few: the medical clinic is now open only 3 afternoons a week where the first week or so it was a 24-hour a day operation. The clothing trailer is open only sporadically to provide winter clothing where in the beginning it was open 8 hours a day. The crisis center is open on a schedule similar to the medical clinic. The Port-A-Potties will leave today. Those were installed around the camp so that the long trip back to cabins would not be necessary. The office, where questions are answered, is now a 9-5, Monday-Saturday operation. In the beginning it had no set hours and people lined up (literally) to have their questions answered--some would say to have their questions not-answered. The post-office is open one hour a day and people still line up there because the post-office is one of the most important places on the campus--that is how FEMA checks arrive and also letters from family and friends.

Monday will be the last day that residents can obtain free bus tickets to wherever they want to go. That means these people will need to leave by Tuesday, 6:15 AM, unless they want to pay for the ride themselves. So, for some, it is crunch time. Got to get the plans made.

For those who are staying in NW Arkansas Thursday and Friday will, hopefully, be big move-out days. Many have their new housing leases signed, have HUD approval of the housing choice, and know that their next 12 months of rent will be paid for them. Now they are awaiting the arrival of their new furniture and they will be ready to go. We have rented three U-Haul type trucks to move people the next few days. We will just be moving personal belongings that have been accumulated while at the camp. The furniture, of course, will be delivered to their new homes.

One of the interesting things I observed during Rose's move-in a couple of weeks ago was that by the end of the day her house was in order, there were no big cartons of dishes, bedding, books, and other stuff filling the house and awaiting unpacking because she had none of these. The family had personal clothing, a few new linens, their new furniture that was already arranged in the house, their dishes, pots and pans, and other kitchen items that had arrived a few days before and were already put away. That was all. Then I look back at what our Arkansas house looked like the day the van unloaded when we moved from California and there is no similarity. It was weeks before the cartons vanished from our house--and I think there is still a couple in the attic that, now nearly two years later, have not been opened. There is a lesson in there somewhere. Now their home is gradually looking more like a home--a place where people live--Erika's bedroom has a poster on the wall. Rose's room has a new lamp by her bedside. There are newspapers and magazines. Roger's dresser top looks like a teenager's dresser. And when I was there yesterday all three beds were made. Mine wasn't.

Rose still has some personal items she wants to retrieve from New Orleans. Things accumulated throughout a lifetime. She has been in contact with her landlords there and they have promised to personally secure her things. Hopefully, the valuable things will still be intact. It is hard to replace a lifetime.

Roger had his first JV football game on Monday. I haven't heard the whole story of the game yet but evidently he didn't just play wide receiver. He actually had an interception. And Siloam won the game. Can't get better than that. His new contact lenses must have worked just fine.

As you know, yesterday was my last day at the camp. Today and tomorrow I will do some things to get ready for our vacation and then we will leave on Friday morning with our destinations Indianapolis and Green Bay with intermediate stops in Champaign, Bloomington and Naperville, Illinois, and around Milwaukee on the way home. We'll be back on October 13 and I plan to go to camp on the 14th. After that I will write one more letter to you about that day, look back on the experience and try to put the whole thing into perspective.

Until then,

Bettie

Saturday, October 15

The Final Chapter

Dear Friends,

The camp is closed. Today, October 15 was supposed to be the final day but it actually happened on Wednesday, October 12. On that morning there were 17 people in the camp. By 1:00 PM the camp was empty. That doesn't mean all of the work is done. Those full-time, temporary city employees, who were hired for the last weeks of the camp to assure that people were relocated in a timely fashion, are still on the job. There are still apartments without furniture and people camping out in them--but at least they are warm! Hopefully these issues will be taken care of next week. There is still paper work to be done, reports to be filed, bills to be paid. The camp is being cleaned and being put in shape for its winter rest.

I, and I am sure, several others are feeling somewhat restless, not knowing exactly what to do now that we are going back to our regular lives. Wendell and I had the last week away and that kind of acted as a buffer between the camp and regular life. But I wish I could have been there for the last day. I was there the first day and I would have liked to have seen it through to the end. I do have some thank you letters to write to people in the churches who stepped up and made my assignment not only easier but also pleasurable. I have often said that the best thing about this experience was getting to meet so many people I would not have otherwise known. In so many ways, this experience made Wendell and me a part of this community where we have lived for two years but were just getting acquainted.

I don't yet have the final statistics but I think that about 100 people stayed in NW Arkansas. I think most will be here at least a year--that is the time the state/federal governments are subsidizing rent and utilities. If people leave their current housing that subsidy will not follow them. I know for many, the pull to return to the hurricane-stricken areas will be strong. After all, it is home. For others, the opportunity to start over will keep them here and they will enhance our communities.

Zack, the lost/stolen lab, has not been seen again. That is the saddest note of the experience. He was such a part of the camp and such a good dog. I know Scott and his family sorely miss him and his loss will be felt for a very long time. When this experience is remembered it will be always accompanied with the thought that this is when Zack was lost.

Rose is still working in her temporary capacity with the city until the program officially shuts down--maybe another week or so. Then I think she will give herself a little break--time to, in her words, "act like an evacuee". She has not done that at all since arriving here. She has been so busy helping others that she has not had a real opportunity to decompress and evaluate all that has happened to her in the past two months. Then she will go job hunting. She got her Social Security card last week so now she can take her driver's test and when that is obtained she can obtain a car--essential for job hunting and getting to work.

Roger is doing very well with the JV team although he has yet to play with the varsity. He had another interception at the last game. We hope to see a JV game very soon. Roger had 3 desires this year: to get contacts (hard to play football with glasses). He got those recently. The second is to get his driver's license--Mom says no way to that. And the third desire he has realized. He has a puppy. She is a white lab mix with a light brown patch over her right eye. They went to Wal-Mart a week ago and someone in the parking lot was giving them away--that happens pretty often around here. So, Rose let him have it. It is better than the wolf he wanted originally! Rose and Erika are enjoying the puppy as well so I think it is a good thing.

Erika continues to make friends. She has had an overnight with one of her new friends and that went well. She is going to help me clean cupboards next Saturday. Rather, she is going to clean my cupboards next Saturday. I don't intend to do any of the work.

You can now find these letters and some pictures at http://www.newstreetchurch.com/ under "News." One of our friends who received the letters has put them on the church's website. That is Downey First Christian Church, Downey, CA, where we served before moving to Arkansas. And, by the way, if you are ever in Southern California on a Sunday, that is a great place to worship.

These letters, that started out just as a way to bring my thoughts together and to help me process what I was experiencing, have turned into more than I ever dreamed. I have no idea how far they have been forwarded. I do know that I have met, either in person or by e-mail, very delightful people who have extended my realm of friends. You have opened your hearts and wallets to Rose and her family. You have found creative ways to assist her and others at the camp. I am amazed. I am humbled.

I intend to keep my group of addresses I call "Hurricane Stories" and I hope to update you occasionally about Rose and her family. And, who knows, there may be other exciting things happening from time to time. We're learning that NW Arkansas is kind of an exciting place to be. So, don't go away, we'll be in touch.

David, our City Administrator about whom I have told you on several occasions, sent this e-mail on Wednesday. It was titled, "Tomorrow we are done." In part, he wrote, "Today was a small microcosm of the issues that we have faced and every day we found a way to 'make it happen'. If you cannot tell, I am feeling every possible emotion from the news (that we will close tomorrow). We did it, and many lives have been forever changed by our sacrifice!!! TO EVERYONE WHO SERVED...YOU ARE MY HEROES."

You may not have been here. I hope these letters brought you closer to the front lines. But you served. Thank you. YOU ARE MY HEROES.

Until then,

Bettie

November, 2005

Epilogue Number 1

Dear Friends:

I can't help but write this to you today: We believe that Lucky Lass' parents have found her!

Shortly after we got her I registered her on Petfinders.com under Katrina Found Pets. I only got two responses, both wanting to adopt her. We said, "Thanks, but no thanks."

Until this week. We received an e-mail from a woman who said she thought Lucky was the dog they lost in Gulfport during the hurricane. A lot of things make sense that tells us that Lucky is probably their Annie.

She said they had to leave in a hurry and planned to return for their 3 dogs. Annie, who is a 5-year-old purebred Wheaten Scottish Terrier and two standard poodles. When they got back Annie was gone. They later found her tag with the important ID information in the backyard and it looked like she had torn it off trying to get away. Their two poodles later died of disease related to Katrina. I'm not surprised. Lucky had a very, very bad bladder infection when we received her.

Cori (Annie's owner) said the neighbors saw two women pick her up from their street a few days after the storm. Two women brought Lucky to a shelter where she was given to our friend from here that was working in the shelter and said, "Please find her a good home." Were they the same women? We do know that the location where the women found her (as they told my friend) was in the same area that Cori says they lived.

Cori said she had been to all of the Gulfport shelters and no one remembered seeing a dog like Annie (even the one Lucky was found in) and she had almost given up before finding our listing on Petfinders. I'm not surprised though, knowing how workers change in the shelters that no one would remember seeing a dog like Annie.

Cori said Annie had a wide black leather collar that "is not appropriate for a little dog like her but she kept pulling her neck out of the cute little collars so this was all she would keep on." Her description of the collar is identical to the one our Lucky had on when she was found. And guess what? We had to keep tightening Lucky's new collar after we got her because she kept pulling out of it! I had taken the old black leather one off because I thought it was an inappropriate collar for such a little dog.

We've been trying to get Lucky to respond to being called "Annie" but she hasn't shown much response. Is that meaningful?

Cori said Annie was sort of overweight. Yeah, so was Lucky. We have her down by over a pound now.

I directed Cori to the Downey First Christian website (http://www.newstreetchurch.com/) under the "News" tab where our friend, Craig Charlton, has posted all of the Hurricane Letters and where there is a picture of Lucky. That picture encouraged Cori even more although our groomer had groomed Lucky the way that Cori, who is just learning to groom, had wanted to accomplish on Annie.

Cori was so excited about the possibility of this being her dog; she plans to come next week to check her out. I think we will know by the dog's response to her.

This is the height of ambivalence. If Lucky is really Annie it will be the perfect ending to a Hurricane story. I guess that is why I put her on Petfinders. But we have become very fond of her (what is there about her not to love?) and will hate to see her go.

Chica, on the other hand, will probably be very, very happy to be the only dog again. They still are not good loose in the house together. I'm not sure they will ever be.

If you would like to see Annie, go to Petfinders.org and on the Katrina page, look under "find a single pet" or something like that and type in 28199 (Annie's number) and you will see her. Sure looks like Lucky, but then all Wheaten Scottish Terrier's may look alike. Check out the collar.

Now why am I writing this instead of just waiting to learn the outcome? Just because I want to tease you a little, I guess, and let you share in our anticipation. Couldn't help myself!

I'll write more another day. Just couldn't wait to tell you this.

Bettie

November 22, 2005

Epilogue #2

Dear Friends,

Annie has found her first family! Cori and her son came yesterday and took Annie (our Lucky) home with them. What a bittersweet time it was for us. As we said before, this would be the perfect ending--their reunion. But for us it was sad. Incredible, how close we became to that little dog in just three months!

The reunion was not quite as we had anticipated. Annie did not run and jump on them when they came. She was not ecstatic like we thought she would be. And that caused them to have some doubts as well. Especially, Chris, Cori's college-age son. He just wasn't sure. See, she has no real identifying marks on her--like a brown spot or a nick in her ear. She looks like most Wheaten Scottish Terriers. She reluctantly did some of the tricks they had taught her. She did not shy away from them--she just wasn't exuberant.

Chris took her for a walk, played with her and when she stood on her back legs to get a doggie bone he said, "Yes, it is her." Cori was convinced by the collar that she had on when we got her. She was sure it was Annie's collar and she said, "In my deepest heart, I know it is her."

So we sent them on their way with Lucky's shampoo, toothbrush, toothpaste, dog food, heartworm preventive meds, and flea preventive. Oh, yes, and her medical records. You can see she had become very ingrained in our lives.

We found out a lot more about how Cori got to us. Seems there is a woman, Sheila, who has taken it upon herself to help people become reunited with their pets. She spends hours each day checking Petfinders and other online registries for lost and found pets trying to make connections. We have no idea where she lives. Cori and I had both registered our dogs on Petfinders and on November 11 she sent Cori an e-mail stating, "Because Annie is white, she might be listed as a West Highland White Terrier." Then she included 4 listings. Ours was one of them.

On the 14th Cori responded to her with this message, "Thanks for checking. We've suffered a long string of disappointments concerning this dog. We had 3 dogs when Katrina hit. Our home had received no storm surge during Camille and the hotel in Florida wouldn't take pets. We boarded up our garage with 3 dogs inside and lots of food and water. The storm blew out the windows and doors and flooded the garage with nearly 3 feet of water. We never found Annie. The two standard poodles died of disease about 3 weeks later. We went to every shelter within 80 miles. We've pretty much given up hope. Several of the ID's that you listed aren't the right animal--we've already contacted them. I sent e-mails to two that I hadn't seen."

This morning Cori sent this e-mail to Sheila and copied it to us: WE HAVE ANNIE!!!!!!!!

> Thanks so much. I will count you with everyone else who has helped along the way! We are so grateful. I have really struggled to regain my equilibrium since the storm. I feel like things will never get back to normal. I finally feel a sense of hope again. I'm hoping that other dogs will still have a chance to be reunited with their families.

It was worthwhile. We feel confident that Lucky is Annie. What we have now is a sense of accomplishment and completion. Without Roni who brought her to Arkansas and without us who took her in, Annie would probably not have survived. Now she is where she belongs and will help her family heal.

Cori was very generous, offering to reimburse us for all we had spent caring for Annie. We declined but suggested that if she wished she might provide some compensation for Roni who is really responsible for Annie's rescue. She was glad to do that and I think Roni will accept it as a gift of gratitude.

Chica seems not to have noticed that Lucky/Annie is gone. She has contained her glee, I guess.

For you pet owners I have one question: Do you think you could identify your pet if it got lost without its tags? I think we could identify Chica and I'm sure Cori thought it would be no problem to identify Annie, but a different haircut makes a big difference and we had cut her hair differently. If they had put in a microchip there would have been no doubt. I had never thought of microchips that way before. I always thought of it in terms of helping a finder locate the pet's owner.

Now I look at it as sort of doggie DNA--how to confirm this is your pet. Also, although they provided good care for Annie they never got rabies vaccine for her thinking that because she was kept on a leash whenever she was out this was unnecessary. They put her at great risk during this crisis because of that decision. Not knowing her vaccination history we had the vet give her a rabies shot last week. So she is good to go for a year in that department. I think Cori and her family will now do the chip thing and, I hope, her next rabies shot.

Oh, yes, Wendell is currently on his way to Rose's house to pick up Friskie. Friskie is a black and white ShihTzu that Rose is keeping awhile for her sister who has also been displaced from New Orleans. We're keeping him for the weekend while Rose, Roger and Erika travel to Dallas for Thanksgiving with other members of her family. Friskie is a darling little dog but we'll only have him for a few days until they return home.

No, we're not in the market for a permanent brother or sister for Chica. Not yet.

Happy Thanksgiving to you all.

Bettie

August 4, 2006

Eleven Months Later

Dear Friends,

As we approach the first anniversary of Hurricanes Katrina and Rita I thought it was time to send to you a review of the past year and update you on how the post-Katrina months have evolved here in Northwest Arkansas.

As with most years, there is a mix of the good and the not-so-good. Sometimes I look back and seem to dwell on the not-so-good. I'm hoping by the time I finish this letter to you I will be more positive about the aftermath of life at the Arkansas Baptist Assembly.

Around 100 evacuee families from the New Orleans devastation decided to stay in NW Arkansas. They were set up in apartments/houses that were completely furnished by FEMA. For a period of time their rent and utilities have been paid. This, of course, was a major assistance to getting back on their feet.

Over the past several months FEMA has cut back their support and, it seems, most of the families are no longer receiving FEMA benefits. As an example, the family that our church adopted from Mississippi is now on its own. However, they are still here and seem to be thriving. Wendell saw them yesterday, just by chance, and the husband/father is still working although he has changed jobs several times during the eleven months he has been here. Jobs are plentiful and he seems to have no problem going from one job to another. He was called back to his current job after being laid off from there a few months back. They have now lived in 3 houses—the first house was found for them by the church and when FEMA decided to pay the rent for the evacuees the owner did not want to go through the hassle of bringing his house up to Housing Authority standards, so they moved to another home that already met the standards. In that situation the landlord required the family to pay the rent up front and then he (the landlord) reimbursed the family when he received the check from FEMA—an unusual arrangement. Anyway, something happened and there was a falling out and the family moved again. Their current home is in a nice neighborhood, the kids are doing well in school and they told Wendell they have no intention of going back to Mississippi. They have chosen to attend a different church.

On the other hand, Rose is still receiving full benefits from FEMA. She is working full-time, still lives in the same house, has made sure that FEMA knows everything that is happening to her and she continually gets her benefits extended with the most recent notification being that her rent and utilities have been authorized through October.

Without a bureaucratic explanation of why one and not the other is still on FEMA's payment schedule our belief is that Rose has been proactive in keeping FEMA updated on her situation, staying in one house, and becoming firmly rooted in the community. But who knows why the government responds the way it does sometimes.

The last I heard the estimate was that 25-30% of the families have returned to New Orleans or have gone other places. The pull back to New Orleans has been great for some even though opportunities have been better here—New Orleans is home.

There were people who stayed here who were probably not law-abiding before they came but perhaps escaped arrest in New Orleans—they just faded into the fabric of the inner city. They have not been able to do that in the higher visibility of a small town in Northwest Arkansas. An evacuee shot a woman in the thigh. He was caught hiding in the vacated apartment of another evacuee. The same woman, a few months later, along with another evacuee, was arrested for selling cocaine—among other drugs. And of course, they are always identified in the media as being Katrina evacuees.

Remember the wedding that took place at the Camp with great publicity? The caterer, florist, wedding coordinator all donated their services to assure that this couple had a great and memorable wedding. The marriage is definitely on the rocks and I doubt that they are still together. The groom called me and asked if there were funds to help him get to Houston—one way. He said she had gone back on drugs and had wiped out their bank account and he had to get away. He was also a past drug user but contended that he was still clean. I arranged for bus fare for him to Houston but he never used it and I don't know where either is now. It was their vacant apartment that the shooter in the previous paragraph ran to when he was trying to escape the police.

So all of those are negative events and they do tend to color one's impressions. Especially, since many of us (me?) may tend to paint everyone with the same brush. But there are just as many, or more, success stories out there.

There is the Seventh Day Adventist grandmother who cares for her young granddaughter and who was adopted by the Seventh Day Adventist community in Gentry (an even smaller town just north of Siloam Springs.) She is very happy with her new environment, her granddaughter is enrolled in the SDA elementary school and her life is so much better than before. The only problematic thing right now is that FEMA wants her to return to New Orleans and live in one of their empty trailers in that area. Needless to say, she doesn't want to do that but may need to for financial reasons. I'm sure the SDA community is trying to work that one out.

And, there is Rose. Rose finally got her driver's license having worked her way through all of the bureaucratic folderol about her identification. We sold her our 1998 Taurus for less than blue book value—paid for by funds that many of you donated for her establishment here. She did not go to work immediately which was, I must admit, frustrating for us at times, but her waiting paid off and she has an excellent job working with Arkansas Work Force. It is a federally funded agency whose main role is matching people to jobs and assuring that people are prepared for jobs. They provide incentives to employers to hire and train workers by paying part of the new employee's salary and the cost of training for a period of several months. Rose's job is to make these connections, working with both employers and potential employees. Of course it doesn't stop there and she finds herself being an advocate for the client in finding health care, housing, transportation (often a big problem in job hunting), and serving as an all-around counselor in helping people get on their feet. Initially, she has worked specifically with Katrina evacuees but that will eventually transition to the general population. She works 3 days in Siloam Springs and 2 days in the I-540 Corridor. It is a great job that fits her skills quite well.

She and the kids are actively involved in the church and community. Rose became a mentor and mother-figure for the African American students at John Brown University last semester and gave them mature leadership in dealing with a lot of issues about growing up Black and just growing up. Period. Her home is always filled with teen-agers from the high school who are Roger's friends or Junior

High friends of Erika's. A lovely young lady invited Roger to the Senior Prom and he cut quite a figure in his tuxedo. Both of the kids went to two weeks of camp this summer on scholarships. Roger went to a Leadership Camp at New Life Ranch, a Christian Camp in this area and Erika went to Christian Camp for teens.

Rose and the kids have been back to New Orleans when they went this spring to Baton Rouge to visit Robert. I think it was a good time to go back and to confirm their decision to stay here was good.

Rose will sing this next week at the Genesis House banquet and fundraiser. Genesis House is our local program for the homeless. As a part of that she will give her testimony about being homeless and the effects of even a temporary homeless state. Her voice is captivating and she has become an integral part of the Worship Team at our church. She is also assisting with a pre-school Sunday School class with Erika as her helper.

We see Rose at church each week and chat with her and occasionally at other times. We talk with her on the phone and exchange e-mail and once in awhile have lunch. But she is becoming independent and has her own circle of friends. All of this is good. We want to be a part of that circle but her independence speaks well for her future. I was looking back over what I had written during the Camp weeks when we asked for your financial support. We had estimated that it would take about $6000 to establish Rose here with what she needed and to help her until she got a job. And you responded so well. When the last gifts had been counted there was between $6000 and $7000. God does provide through His people.

The first part of the year was filled with awards, banquets and accolades for the Team that put together the care of the evacuees at the Camp. It became almost embarrassing, there was such an outpouring of gratitude and toward the end, even though it was nice, most were hoping it would soon be over. There was lunch with Governor and Mrs. Huckabee at the Governor's mansion on Valentine's Day, there was the recognition by the local Chamber of Commerce and the beautiful event and special award from the American Red Cross. But perhaps the most significant was the New Orleans banquet given in our honor by the evacuees themselves (organized by Rose, of course). Talk about soul food!

There have been changes in the camp itself. I haven't returned to the site but I understand that any damage that was caused to the facility was repaired through funds provided by the government. The camp also received a per-diem for each person cared for during the operation. This per diem exceeded their expenses and so they have been able to do some much needed upgrading of the Camp. Well deserved.

Remember Zack, the Labrador retriever who disappeared during the camp? His body was found not too far from camp, in the wooded area. He had not been shot and it was feared he had been poisoned. To my knowledge no culprit has been found. This was very sad. His owner, Scott the Camp Manager, has left his job with the camp.

I can't close without telling you our own personal dog stories. As you know, Lucky (nee Annie) was returned to her original owners in early November. According to them she fit right back into family life as though she had never been away. We recently received an e-mail from them with bad news, however. Lucky-Annie has bladder cancer and may need surgery. They told us that this condition is fairly common to the breed and has nothing to do with her Katrina experience. However, I have to wonder if this was brewing when she was here and that was part of the reason we had such trouble clearing her bladder infection. At least she is with a loving family who will provide the best care for her.

And we now have Daisy. She came to us early this year. Just showed up very hungry and very sweet. So we fed her, then named her, then had her spayed, vaccinated—all those things—all of the time telling ourselves that we didn't need another dog and we would find her a good home. She is still with us and we are enjoying her youth and enthusiasm. She is a young—probably just over a year old—mostly German Shepherd. She weighs in at about 45-50 pounds. She and Chica actually play some with each other and I think Chica's acceptance of her is because Daisy stays outdoors and Chica has the house—a mistake we made with Lucky, asking Chica to share her house with another dog.

So those are the highlights of eleven months post-Katrina. The story will continue to unroll as the years go by. The experience will be with us in our memories forever and I hope that is how it will stay—a memory—something that we will never have to do again in real time.

Our continued thanks to you for standing with us in so many ways during this year—prayerfully, financially, encouraging all of the way. We are family and we adore the relationship.

Sincerely,

Bettie

July, 2010

Five Years After The Storm

Rose and I met for lunch today. We sat at a window table at Emelia's in downtown Siloam Springs. I had just completed a morning of volunteering at Genesis House, our day shelter for homeless in the area and Rose was on her lunch hour, or hour and a half, as it turned out. We both agreed that we should do this more often but life gets in the road and time for both of us seems to go by too rapidly.

I chose Emelia's as our meeting place because, not only do they have good food, but I thought it would be a quieter place to talk and catch up. My motives were not completely innocent. I wanted Rose's input about what to write in this section. She, more than anyone else I know, has had her life change since the winds and floods struck New Orleans almost five years ago.

But I will start with our town. Siloam Springs is different in 2010. Five years ago we were growing and thriving with the rest of Northwest Arkansas. Employers were searching for employees and eagerly recruited workers from among the Katrina evacuees. Unemployment was at a record low. Today several key businesses have had multiple layoffs. Franklin Electric which was a major employer has closed its plant and taken its business elsewhere. Real estate sales ground to a halt. Before this happened, however, the town grew to 13,900, according to the population signs as you come into town and the mid-decade census.

But there are signs that the economy is improving. The electorate voted to build a much needed high school, replacing the current old, out-dated, inadequate building. The first class will graduate from the new building in 2012. The city-owned hospital was sold to a for-profit group and part of the deal is that there will be a new hospital in a few years. JBU has opened a new dorm, built a new business building and will soon complete a new sports arena and a performing arts center.

Downtown Siloam Springs—that is the area that a lot of towns refer to as "historic"—has come alive again with new specialty shops and a feeling of anticipation. Emelia's is a new restaurant downtown with a Mediterranean focus (can you believe?) actual cloth table coverings and housed in a former car dealership. Books on Broadway opened and is an inviting spot to read and visit. Local Flair features and sells the work of local artists, There is Creative Corner for craft supplies and classes, a florist, an Italian pizzeria, and Heather Hill has opened a boutique featuring her amazing children's clothing line. Then out on Highway 412 Lowe's has opened, so has Tractor Supply and Aldi is under construction.

David is still our City Administrator. He continues to lead the city through both good and tough times and does a good job of it. He was one of my heroes during Katrina and he still is.

The sign at the entrance still reads "Arkansas Baptist Assembly", the campground which housed the Katrina evacuees. But things have changed there as well. In late 2006 the Arkansas Baptist Convention voted to allow the Arkansas Baptist Assembly to become its own non-profit agency with its own Board of Directors. Several upgrades are being planned including a new dining hall, the upgrading of dorms with heat and air conditioning and the building of a gym/indoor track facility.

The family our church adopted following the hurricane has gone back to New Orleans. Wendell recently learned that the husband/father is working as a cook in a seafood restaurant. Our hope is that the restaurant will survive the effects of the oil spill so that they will not be uprooted again.

Mike Huckabee was our governor five years ago and showed his wisdom and compassion during that time. Another one of the heroes in my book. Several have told me that the first time they heard his name was in my daily journal but they came to like what they learned about him. He, of course, came to national prominence when he was a presidential candidate in 2008 and everyone knows what has happened to him since then and can watch him every weekend on Fox News or listen to his daily radio broadcasts. And 2012 is not too far away.....

We have lost contact with Lucky/Annie's owners in Mississippi. We hope that she is well. We keep her picture on the wall along with Daisy, Chica, and our new addition, Turbo. We lost our precious Chica this June after living a year with kidney failure. She was over 15 when she died and had brought us immense joy as our very first ever pet. Last year Turbo literally walked into our house one Friday night and never left. The vet told us that he was under four months old at the time. We sort of looked for an owner but no one claimed him so he became ours and has become a companion/irritant for Daisy. He is probably a rat terrier although some people think he is a Jack Russell. The name is descriptive of his early behavior although as he has now passed his first birthday he is considerably calmer. He is quite athletic and his long legs carry him easily through a hula hoop. He is white with brown and black markings and a very intelligent face. Daisy became a calendar girl a few years ago when she was one of the twelve pets selected by readers of our newspaper to have a page in their annual calendar. She was Miss February. Actually the votes were cast at a quarter a vote and the money went to the paper's literacy program and to the Humane Society. We have a lot of generous friends as was proven during our post-Katrina experience.

I read recently that there are still over 900 Katrina families in Arkansas. Rose estimates that there are only five remaining in Siloam Springs but probably ten times that in Northwest Arkansas. It is difficult to get an accurate count since, to my knowledge, no agency keeps record. Those who have stayed have become part of the fabric of their community. Those who returned to Mississippi or Louisiana have returned home and those who went to other places have hopefully found opportunities there.

Rose and her family have definitely become a part of our community. Rose's focus has been her kids and the effort and resources it takes to get them launched into adulthood. She has done a good job. She still lives in the house that we found for her five years ago and she still works for Arkansas Workforce although she has been given increasing responsibilities in the Siloam office. She is completely on her own now, financially speaking, as all of the FEMA support has ended. Sometimes it is a struggle but she has always figured out a way to make the ends stretch far enough to meet. In the early years she was very active in community affairs, high school booster groups, and could be seen at most events. These days she studies and studies, working hard to complete her bachelor degree in human relations from the University of Arkansas. Occasionally we get to hear her sing, but not often enough. Rose has a huge personality and when she walks into a room you can feel that room change. People gravitate toward her and want to be acknowledged by her. A fascinating phenomenon to observe.

Roger took high school by storm. He has a lot of his mother's personality; add his athletic skills and he became a pretty big man on campus. He played varsity football his last two years as a wide receiver and was the favorite receiver for his best friend, the quarterback. The team was very good and qualified for the state playoffs both years. Roger won All-Conference awards and had his name and picture in the local paper a lot. I thought his high school sports career was over after his senior year of football but then he decided to go out for basketball. I thought that should have been his major sport all along—that is until I saw him play his first game. Only then did I learn he had never played organized basketball. Oh, my! He looked lost and confused on the floor, hardly knowing what to do with the ball. All of that was history by the time the conference season rolled around. He had become a confident player and was one of the starting five, especially shining with his defensive skills. And he was the emotional leader of the team. It took on an extra burst of energy when Roger was on the court. The team was excellent and they won the state title in 2008 with Roger being named to the All Tournament Team. Now he is at Arkansas Tech University, a school of about 7500, where his major is communications. He is there on a partial football scholarship, additional scholarships and financial aid. He is doing well in school, has a job there this summer while taking a class, and hopes to play major minutes for the team this fall. We'll be there again this year for his home games. He will be a junior. He is learning some of the hard lessons in life, especially about money management. He has 3,360 friends on Facebook which tells you a little about his social life.

Erika is a charming young woman who just celebrated her 17th birthday. She will be a senior this year and will graduate mid-year. She will start to college then but has yet to decide on a major. It has been a joy to watch her mature and to see those flashes of the woman she will become. She has wrestled with being Roger's "little sister", but is coming into her own with her own personality. It helps that Roger is a couple of hours away. But their relationship is good.

When I asked Rose if she was glad she stayed here, she just laughed at me. I don't believe she has ever doubted her decision and is sure it was best for the kids. It has not always been an easy transition but this family is resilient and I have no doubt that they will continue to thrive.

Wendell and I continue to be involved at church, especially with missions outreach. Wendell works for H and R Block each tax season which is good—gives him a scheduled activity during those winter months. During the summer he is the main caretaker of our 2 ¼ acres in the country. I work two days at Community Clinic as the Health Educator. I did that for a year or so as a volunteer and then a couple of years ago it became a paying position. I enjoy it. It keeps me in nursing and I feel it serves the community as our client base is primarily from low income and uninsured people.

I look back at those six weeks in the fall of 2005 with wonderment. I find that in conversation I frequently refer to the "Katrina Camp." Our involvement helped cement us to this community where we had lived for only a couple of years. Katrina taught us many lessons: how a community can come together during a crisis, how territorialism can be overcome to get the job done, how people who have never done something like this can actually learn on the fly and make it work, how generous people are when they have the opportunity to help, how resilient the human spirit can be and, most of all, how God hears our prayers before they are even uttered.

Five years after Katrina we still feel its imprint on this community. That is a good thing. We hope we are never called upon to do this again. But if we are, we will. And we will do it better because of Katrina.

Rose, Roger and Erika shortly after moving into their new Siloam home
September, 2005

Lucky Lass—The Before Picture

Lucky Lass—The After Picture

*Lucky Lass with her First Family the day she went home
to Mississippi*

*Me, Chica, Lucky Lass and Wendell the last day Lucky lived in
Arkansas*

Rose and Roger celebrating after Siloam's State Basketball Championship Game, 2008

Roger and Erika, 2009

Rose and Erika, 2010

www.ingramcontent.com/pod-product-compliance
Lightning Source LLC
Chambersburg PA
CBHW031235280526
45784CB00004B/1587